Mont. : 1965-1994) University of Montana (Missoula

The University of Montana Report of the President

Mont. : 1965-1994) University of Montana (Missoula

The University of Montana Report of the President

ISBN/EAN: 9783743325166

Manufactured in Europe, USA, Canada, Australia, Japa

Cover: Foto ©ninafisch / pixelio.de

Manufactured and distributed by brebook publishing software
(www.brebook.com)

Mont. : 1965-1994) University of Montana (Missoula

The University of Montana Report of the President

BULLETIN

OF THE

UNIVERSITY OF MONTANA

ISSUED BI-MONTHLY - MISSOULA, MONTANA

WHOLE NUMBER 68   PRESIDENT'S REPORT SERIES No. 15

DECEMBER, 1910

PRESIDENT'S REPORT, 1910

Entered August 24, 1901, at Missoula, Montana, as Second Class Matter, under Act of
Congress, July 16, 1894

UNIVERSITY OF MONTANA

ANNUAL REPORT OF THE PRESIDENT

DECEMBER 5, 1910.

To the Montana State Board of Education:

Gentlemen:—In accordance with the requirements of the statutes, I have the honor to submit herewith the sixteenth annual report of the State University, this being my third report as President.

GENERAL PROGRESS SINCE DECEMBER 1, 1909.

The University has made marked progress in several directions during the past year.

The Faculty has been strengthened by changes and additions of efficient instructors. Five of the staff who were on the rolls one year ago are no longer with the University. Seven new appointments have been made. One professor and one instructor who were studying abroad on leave of absence have returned to their duties, while one instructor is now absent for a similar purpose.

The laboratories and libraries have been improved by moderate expenditures for equipment and books. Large as the unsatisfied requests of all departments for improvements of this nature are, the steady progress made recently is hopeful.

New developments in the organization of departments of Physics, Botany and Forestry have given the work in these fields a much needed impetus.

University Extension courses by lectures and correspondence have been inaugurated with excellent results. Similarly the new Short Course in Forestry, given in January, February and March, brought to the University a group of earnest students who could not enroll in regular collegiate courses.

The period of transition to the advanced standard of a purely collegiate and professional institution brought one of its consequences in decreased registration of students, but the present semester shows an increased attendance of twenty-one per cent (rising from 145 to 176) over the enrollment of the first semester of the preceding year. It may safely be concluded that the University has entered upon a period of pronounced growth in registration. This is partly a natural result of the general

N. B.—The President's Report of December 1, 1909, was not printed. Certain sections are now printed in Appendix II.

growth of the state, but it follows especially from the better standards adopted and enforced in accordance with the policy of your honorable board. The people of Montana will appreciate and use the facilities of their State University just in proportion as they know that their sons and daughters will find in it instruction of the best quality.

Last year's faculty legislation for the liberalizing of the collegiate courses has been administered with apparent success. About three years more (or one college generation) are required to give the proper basis of experience for judgment of the composite elective, group and major department system now in force. It would appear, however, that students find satisfaction in its reasonable freedom of election, controlled by official faculty advisers. The members of the faculty get better work from students because classes are not composed of coerced learners. The requirement that the greater part of the hours of Junior and Senior years must be given to some one major department likewise stimulates the interest of students and the scholarly zeal of instructors.

THE UNIVERSITY FACULTY.

The faculty as at present constituted is as follows:

Clyde A. Duniway, Ph. D., President.

William M. Aber, A. B., Professor of Latin and Greek.

Frederick C. Scheuch, B. M. E., A. C., Professor of Modern Languages.

Morton J. Elrod, Ph. D., Professor of Biology.

Frances Corbin, B. L., Professor of Literature.

William D. Harkins, Ph. D., Professor of Chemistry.

Jesse P. Rowe, Ph. D., Professor of Geology.

William F. Book, Ph. D., Professor of Psychology and Education.

Joseph H. Underwood, Ph. D., Professor of History and Economics.

Louis C. Plant, M. S., Professor of Mathemtaics.

Arthur W. Richter, M. M. E., Professor of Engineering.

Joseph E. Kirkwood, Ph. D., Professor of Botany and Forestry.

George F. Reynolds, Ph. D., Professor of English and Rhetoric.

Gustav L. Fischer, Professor of Music.

Robert N. Thompson, B. S., Assistant Professor of Physics.

E. M. Shealey, M. M. E., Assistant Professor of Engineering.

Robert H. Cary, B. S., Director of Physical Culture.

Eloise Knowles, M. A., Instructor in Fine Arts.

Mary Stewart, A. B., Instructor in English and Dean of Women. (On leave of absence).

Eugene F. A. Carey, B. S., Instructor in Mathematics.

Mabel R. Smith, M. A., Instructor in Public Speaking and in Physical Culture. (Acting Dean of Women).

William R. Plew, M. S., Instructor in Engineering.

J. Howard Stoutemyer, Ph. D., Instructor in History and Education.

J. W. Hill, M. A., Instructor in Chemistry.

Helen F. Walker, B. L., Ph. B., Instructor in English and German.

James B. Speer, B. A., Registrar and President's Secretary.

Gertrude Buckhouse, B. S., Librarian.

Margery W. Feighner, B. A., Assistant Librarian.

Promotions in rank took effect in September in the cases of Joseph E. Kirkwood, made Professor instead of Assistant Professor of Botany and Forestry; George F. Reynolds, made Professor instead of Assistant Professor of English and Rhetoric; James B. Speer, made Registrar and President's Secretary instead of Acting Registrar and President's Secretary; Robert N. Thompson, made Assistant Professor instead of Instructor in Physics.

Salaries of the Faculty have been steadily increased in moderate amounts. The maximum salary now paid to a professor is $2,250, while an assistant professor may receive $1,800, and instructors receive from $1,000 to $1,350, varying with length of service. The subject is one that must recur with regularity in annual reports, and I wish to repeat my recommendations that considerations of justice to these underpaid public servants and of regard to the interests of advanced scholarship should sanction substantial increases in the standard of salaries. To the degree that maintenance appropriations will permit, the Executive Board of the University is disposed to act on this principle in dealing with the faculty. More specific recommendations may be expected next June when appointments for 1911-12 are presented for your consideration.

The names of those members of the faculty who were on the roll during part or all of the academic year 1909-10, but are not in the service of the University at present, are as follows:

Walter Arthur, B. S., Instructor in Chemistry, whose appointment terminated on September 1, 1910.

Alvin J. Cox, Ph. D., Acting Professor of Chemistry, who returned to his position in the Bureau of Science of the Philippine Islands last June, on the expiration of his leave of absence.

Allston Dana, A. B., B. S., Instructor in Engineering, who

declined a re-appointment with promotion because he wished to go into engineering practice.

James W. Rhodes, Director of Physical Culture, whose appointment terminated on September 1, 1910.

J. K. Witzman, Professor of Music, who was temporarily employed during the absence of Professor Whitaker.

Mrs. Blanche Whitaker, Professor of Music, who was necessarily irregular in her employment because of illness in her family, and who declined a re-appointment after many years of faithful and efficient service.

The Executive Board has made five appointments since the June meeting of this Board. These are submitted at this time under standing regulations for your approval:

Gustav L. Fischer, Professor of Music.

J. W. Hill, Instructor in Chemistry, beginning September 1, 1910.

William R. Plew, Instructor in Engineering, beginning September 1, 1910.

J. Howard Stoutemyer, Instructor in History and Education, beginning September 1, 1910.

Helen F. Walker, Instructor in English and German, beginning September 1, 1910.

Mr. Gustav L. Fischer, Professor of Music, is a native of Germany. Reared in a musical atmosphere, he received a thorough musical training in Hamburg, Weimar, Buckeburg, and Frankfurt. In Weimar Mr. Fischer played as a student in the Court Orchestra; also in Buckeburg, he played in the Court Orchestra and studied with violin virtuoso, Professor R. Sahla and with the Court Pianist, Clemenz Schultze. In America Mr. Fischer has been a member of the celebrated Theodore Thomas Orchestra, the St. Louis Choral Symphony Society, the World's Fair Symphony Orchestra and other organizations. As a teacher of piano and string instruments, Mr. Fisher has a long experience. He also is a composer, the music of the Montana Prize State Song being one of his compositions.

Mr. J. W. Hill, Instructor in Chemistry, is a native of Hampton, New Brunswick. His higher education began with one year in the Provincial Normal School at Fredericton, which was followed by the completion of a course at the University of New Brunswick with the degree of Bachelor of Arts, with honors in Chemistry and Natural Science. In 1907, he received the degree of Master of Arts from his alma mater on completion of a course in Agricultural Analysis and Biology. Entering Yale University on a graduate scholarship in 1908, Mr. Hill received the degree of Master of Arts from the University in 1909. Last year he was assistant in Chemistry in that institution. He also had teaching experience in his specialty at the University of New Brunswick and the Rutherford Institution of New Haven.

Mr. William R. Plew, Instructor in Engineering, comes to Montana from Rose Polytechnic Institute of Indiana. For three years he had been a successful instructor in Civil Engineering in that institution, from which he graduated in 1907, with the degree of Bachelor of Science in Civil Engineering. In 1909 he received from his alma mater the advanced degree of Master of Science in Civil Engineering. His practical experience was obtained in the service of the Pons Bridge Company, the city of Terre Haute, and the village of Palestine, as well as in various capacities as consulting engineer.

Mr. J. Howard Stoutemyer, Instructor in History and Education, obtained his earlier collegiate training at Kalamazoo College, Michigan. He holds also the degrees of Bachelor of Arts from the University of Chicago, and Doctor of Philosophy from Clark University. For the present Dr. Stoutemyer will divide his time about equally between elementary classes in History and those in Education.

Miss Helen Walker, Instructor in German and English, holds the degree of Bachelor of Letters from Oberlin College and Bachelor of Philosophy from the University of Chicago. She has had several years of successful teaching of modern languages, coming to Montana from the headship of that department in the high school of Clinton, Iowa. Miss Walker's present appointment is for the first semester, partly as a substitute for Miss Stewart, who is studying in Berlin and Paris while on leave of absence.

EQUIPMENT OF LABORATORIES AND LIBRARY.

In the calendar year just closing, about $8,500 have been expended in the equipment of departments, including the library. These expenditures have included only small sums for supplies, books and apparatus requiring most of the money. The departments have thus been enabled to provide better facilities for instruction of higher grade, yet candid consideration of the actual conditions will lead to the conclusion that the facilities now in use need very substantial additions, larger in amount than have hitherto been provided. The detailed reports of the heads of departments on the needs of their work give convincing proof that the University can meet the obligations of modern scientific scholarship only by the adoption of such a policy.

ORGANIZATION AND EXPANSION OF DEPARTMENTS.

As foreshadowed in the report of last year, division of departments has recently been made in two instances. The former combined Department of Physics and Geology has been separated into a Department of Physics and a Department of Geology. The inclusive single Department of Biology is divided into the two Departments of Biology and Botany and Forestry.

The special field of Dr. Rowe in Geology and Mineralogy is now receiving proper attention because he is able to give his whole time to its development by instruction and investigation. Physics then receives the attention from Assistant Professor Thompson, which its importance as a fundamental science deserves in collegiate and professional courses alike.

So great a variety of subjects was comprehended under Biology that its subdivision waited only for a proper opportunity. The appointment of Dr. Kirkwood has brought its logical result in the separate administration of Botany and Forestry. General Biology remains all too inclusive, for the important field of Physiology can be but imperfectly covered by a professor who must provide at least elementary courses in Zoology, Entomology and Bacteriology. Nevertheless Dr. Elrod is now enabled to offer more satisfactory courses, while Dr. Kirkwood is giving a proper development to Botany and to scientific Forestry.

The Department of History and Economics should be subdivided just as soon as circumstances will permit, and the same statement holds good for the Department of Philosophy and Education. The importance of the subjects embraced in the departments, the breadth of work which professors must endeavor to teach, the demands of numbers of students, all unite to urge the suggested subdivisions. The appointment of an Instructor in History and Education this year has relieved the situation temporarily, but this action is inadequate.

SHORT COURSE IN FORESTRY.

Last December your honorable board sanctioned the principle of a proposed arrangement between the University and District No. 1 of the United States Forest Service by which officers of the Service and the Faculty of the University were to co-operate in giving a special Forestry Course of three months at the University. This course was planned to meet the special needs of forest rangers and was valuable for students desiring to enter the profession or to improve their practical knowledge. The subjects of instruction were Dendrology, Silviculture, Forest Management, Surveying and Mapping, Geology and Mineralogy, Lumbering, Measurements, Timber Sales and Planting, Grazing, Practical Mathematics and Office Administration. Laboratory practice and field demonstration emphasized the practical nature of the whole course.

At this point I should make cordial acknowledgement of the action of the State College of Agriculture in abandoning its announced courses in Forestry when it became clear that the location of the headquarters of District No. 1 in Missoula made the University the logical place for work in this subject.

Admission to the short course was permitted without the certificates and examinations required of students entering one of the regular courses. Fifty special students enrolled in the first week in January, forty-six of these being United States forest rangers on furlough. It was a most unusual body of earnest students, men with a direct professional purpose eager to get the advantages open to them.

Most unfortunately the status of the rangers absent from the forests on furlough for the purpose of improving their professional efficiency became involved in political controversies regarding the administration of Mr. Pinchot. A comptroller's ruling withdrew from the rangers the privilege of receiving their salaries while attending the course. This unforseen change in the terms upon which the men had come to the University obliged thirty of them to withdraw from the course at the end of the third week of instruction. The other twenty continued their special courses, at considerable financial sacrifice, mostly until the end of the period of three months, according to the original plan.

It is the unanimous opinion alike of the officers of the Forest Service and of the Faculty that the Short Course in Forestry was so great a success that it ought to be continued. Conferences are now being conducted with the Forester and District Forester to procure the largest co-operation consistent with the rulings of the Secretary of Agriculture for the second session of the course during the ensuing January, February and March.

Announcements at this time would be premature, but it seems clear that the University should again organize and give its Short Course in Forestry. There is every reason to believe that the course will be attended by considerable numbers of students, who will come to seek the advantages of the University supplemented by the technical professional instruction of officers of the Service.

The cordial thanks of the University are due to the special lecturers in Forestry who taught in the former course. These were:

William B. Greeley, District Forester, District No. 1; A. B., University of California, 1901; M. F., Yale University, 1904.

C. H. Adams, Assistant District Forester in charge of Grazing, District No. 1.

Edward C. Clifford, Chief of Planting, District No. 1; B. S., University of Maine, 1904; University of Michigan, 1906.

G. A. Fitzwater, Deputy Supervisor, Absaroka National Forest; M. F., Yale University, 1908.

J. F. Jardine, Grazing Expert of the Forest Service.

M. J. Knowles, State Veterinarian.

R. G. Pond, Deputy Supervisor, Missoula, National Forest Biltmore Forest School, 1906.

W. G. Weigle, Supervisor, Coeur d'Alene National Forest; Yale Forest School, 1904.

SPECIAL COURSE IN ELEMENTARY LAW.

During the present semester a general culture course in Elementary Law is being given at the University with the assistance of twelve prominent lawyers of the state. This course is not intended to take rank as professional training, but is a valuable introduction to the study of law and a means of imparting general information in an important field. The lectures have been open to the public and have been well attended. In a sense, the giving of a course in Elementary Law is meant to be preliminary to the establishment of a new Department of Law, which should come into existence at the University next September.

I wish to record here, with sincere acknowledgement of their courtesy and unrequited service, the names of the special lecturers to whom the University owes this course. They are:

Chief Justice Theodore Brantly; subject, "Extraordinary Remedies" and "Jurisdiction of Courts."

Judge E. K. Cheadle; subject, "The Common Law."

Judge John B. Clayberg; subject, "Water Rights and Mining Laws."

Mr. A. L. Duncan; subject, "Real Property."

Mr. J. J. Marquette; subject, "Corporation Law."

Mr. T. C. Marshall; subject, "Equity."

Mr. E. C. Mulroney; subject, "Administration of Criminal Law."

Judge H. L. Myers; subject, "Pleading and Practice" and "The Common Law."

Mr. Welling Napton; subject, "Functions of Jurors."

Mr. H. H. Parsons; subject, "Contracts."

Mr. J. E. Patterson; subject, "Torts."

Mr. J. H. Tolan; subject. "Probate Law."

Lectures in the course have also been given by Professor Underwood on "Courts of the United States and Their Jurisdiction," and by the President on "International Law."

SPECIAL COURSE IN PUBLIC HYGIENE.

A course similar in purpose to the one just described will be given during the second semester upon "Public Hygiene." Fifteen prominent physicians, including Dr. Thomas D. Tuttle, Secretary of the State Board of Health, and Dr. M. E. Knowles, State Veterinarian, have generously accepted invitations to give lectures in the course. Certain elements will then be supplied by Dr. Elrod in the field of Bacteriology and by Dr. Harkins in the field of Sanitary Chemistry.

It is to be hoped that the stimulation of interest in this important field may soon be followed by the development of a strong pre-medical course in the University. A medical school need not be organized for some years yet. but the first two years of a medical course may be provided with great advantage to the state.

UNIVERSITY EXTENSION COURSES.

The financial estimates of a later section of this report include a recommendation for a special appropriation for the development of a University Extension Department. A modest but successful beginning of work of this character has already been made. From January to April last, courses of lectures, besides numerous single lectures in various towns, were given successfully in Missoula, Deer Lodge, Bozeman, Billings, Helena and Butte. A total of 544 persons were regularly enrolled in the eight courses given in these six cities. Arrangements have been concluded thus early in the present year for similar courses in Missoula, Helena, Butte. Philipsburg, Victor. Inquiries indicate also that lecture courses are to be given soon in Great Falls, Billings, Bozeman, Columbus, Stevensville, Hamilton and Kalispell. Likewise the preliminary announcements have been made for a system of Correspondence Courses, including work in the Departments of Latin. German. English, Literature, Education. Economics, Biology, Forestry. Physics, Mathematics and Engineering. All these plans require financial support for their development if they are to result in diffusing their benefits throughout the state. The justification of the existence of the University is that it should disseminate knowledge as widely as possible among its proper constituency, the whole people of the state. Extension Lectures and Correspondence Courses may be made to bring the University in the future to the direct service of a majority of our population. This important field of education should not be left to commercial institutions.

Extension lecture courses may be had in the Departments of History and Economics, by Professor Underwood and the President; English, by Professor Reynolds; Psychology and Education, by Professor Book; Geology, by Professor Rowe; Biology, by Professor Elrod; Botany and Forestry, by Professor Kirkwood; Physics, by Professor Thompson.

ENTRANCE REQUIREMENTS AND RELATIONS WITH HIGH SCHOOLS.

One year ago I reported to this board the adoption of new faculty regulations upon entrance requirements for the regular courses of the University. The essential point of new system was the recognition of any full four years course in an accredited high school as entitling a graduate to unconditional entrance. The former list of required subjects was abolished, and the transition from high school to collegiate classes was to be made directly without artificial barriers.

This legislation by the University was supplemented and completed last June when this board adopted new regulations upon courses of study in accredited high schools, reported by a committee composed of Superintendent Largent, Superintendent Harmon and the President of the University. These regulations are as follows:

"Accredited High Schools of the State of Montana shall maintain one or more four years' courses of study, in all of which the following subjects shall be constant elements for the minimum amounts indicated:

   (1)   English Composition and Literature, 4 years, 4 units;
   (2)   Languages other than English, 2 years, 2 units;
   (3)   Mathematics, 2 years, 2 units;
   (4)   Science, 1 year, 1 unit;
   (5)   History, 1 year, 1 unit;
   Total in prescribed subjects, 10 units.

"The authorities of each accredited school in their discretion may make suitable combinations of the constant elements with selections from the following list of subjects in amounts sufficient to constitute one or more full four years' courses of not less than fifteen units:

   (1)   Languages other than English, 4 years, 4 units.
   (2)   Mathematics, 2 years, 2 units.
   (3)   Science, 3 years, 3 units.
   (4)   History (including Civics and Economics), 3 years, 3 units.
   (5)   Drawing, 2 years, 2 units.
   (6)   Commercial Subjects, 4 years, 6 units.
   (7)   Industrial Subjects, 4 years, 6 units."

High School principals have received the completion of the new system with great satisfaction. They now have all reasonable freedom in the organization of their courses of study to meet the needs of their communities, while still preparing their graduates for University courses. They no longer feel in Montana the resentment against the domination of higher institutions such as found vigorous expression at the National Educational Association meeting in Boston last summer.

The University on its part is willing to have its doors open freely to all who have completed a four years preparatory course. Some difficulties appear in the adjustment of individuals to technical courses. Students who may have omitted Physics or the more advanced secondary Mathematics, have a handicap in the University technical departments. If high school pupils and principals could foresee accurately the future courses of the former, this lack of adjustment would cease. But this is impossible, for many young men change their minds about their life work between the ages of seventeen and nineteen. There is less real waste in requiring a few students to repair omissions in their preparation after they reach the University than in constraining many to take subjects against which they are in continuous mental rebellion.

FUTURE EDUCATIONAL POLICY

Realizing that you properly expect from the President of the University not merely administration of the institution under the existing conditions, but prevision of its educational future, let me attempt an answer to a question not infrequently asked: "What general educational policy should the University pursue?" The attitude of mind with which the inquiry should be faced has been given by implication in preceding sections of this report. A State University should first be a good standard teaching college. It should then maintain professional departments of high efficiency. It should foster the love of sound learning, the spirit of scholarship, the scientific love of truth, in all its members. It should make of the young men and women who come to its halls healthy, well informed, well trained citizens. To as many as can take the best, it must offer the ripest fruits of disinterested scholarship. The practical and vocational aspects of its courses must satisfy the legitimate demands of present day society for personal efficiency. Yet the University must transcend all these functions, for it must furnish leadership in all the higher fields of intellectual, professional, industrial, and social activity. We, who are its trustees and its officers, must seek to constitute its faculty, to maintain and equip its departments, to extend its beneficient activity, to these great ends.

Whenever reasonable opportunities present themselves for the use of the resources of the state for the good of the people through higher education, it is wise patriotism to advocate and procure such use. The general educational policy of the University should be to maintain good standards and to offer their benefits generously to the sons and daughters of all the people.

ESTABLISHMENT OF NEW DEPARTMENTS.

At this time I recommend some definite action by your honorable board looking to the prompt establishment of a new Department of Law, a Summer School, and a Department of University Extension. The last named has been treated in an earlier section of this report and needs no further comment at this time.

A Department of Law is urgently needed to satisfy a demand which makes itself felt by the numerous inquiries coming to my office from prospective students. Large numbers of young men of this state, and not a few from other states, would welcome the opportunity to study in such a department. Montana citizens are compelled to leave the state for a legal education, and surely this condition should be remedied, now that the University is maintaining proper collegiate standards. It is my judgment that the establishment of a Department of Law would bring to the University in the next five years nearly as large an addition to the present student body as the total enrollment of men who are in the institution. The proposal to provide professional instruction in Law is endorsed by large numbers of practicing lawyers in all sections of the state. For these reasons, thus briefly expressed, I hope that you will endorse this proposal and recommend the appropriation for its support.

I recommend also, to your favorable consideration, the proposal to establish a Summer School to begin its work next summer. This step commends itself to any one familiar with the striking service rendered by summer schools in other universities all over the country. Such a conviction is strengthened by study of the special conditions in Montana, where large numbers of teachers are eager to improve their professional equipment by study in educational centers. The University has the equipment in buildings, faculty, laboratories, and library, to meet these demands. One can not but be struck by the waste involved in allowing its organization and its valuable plant to lie unused for one-fourth of the year. While protecting the faculty in vacation rights which experience accords to them, it will be feasible to organize and administer a well-equipped Summer School, in which a majority of the departments will be represented each year, for an expenditure of about $5,000—the sum recommended as a special appropriation for this purpose.

The Summer School which is in contemplation would not be designed to afford delinquent and ill-prepared students a means to make up their deficiencies. The enterprising and far-sighted student would utilize it to shorten his collegiate course or his professional training. It would appeal mainly to those persons who are not able to gratify their ambitions by taking full university courses. A leading feature of its organization should be the special employment of a few professors from sister universities and of lecturers on pedagogical methods from among the educational leaders of the state.

NEW BUILDINGS AND CAMPUS EXTENSION.

A pressing need for the men of the student body is a dormitory building. The conditions of student life for women students are excellent. Those whose parents do not live in Missoula reside in a comfortable dormitory upon the campus, under the care of an advisory Dean of Women. There they get board and room at cost, for $25.00 per month. The young men have a much more difficult problem to face. The cost of living to them may vary from $30.00 to $35.00 per month, depending upon the comfort of their quarters and their accessibility. Those who are taken into the fraternities and live in their co-operative club houses may reduce this expense to about $25.00 per month. Others who are willing to combine collegiate life with close economy in undesirable circumstances may be able to limit their necessary expenditures below even this figure. There is no greater discouragement to the coming of ambitious men to the University than the relatively high cost of living which prevails in Missoula. Aside from this matter of expense, a dormitory would provide a better means of supervising the welfare of the young men who leave their homes to take up residence in an unfamiliar city with unaccustomed freedom from the conservative influences of their homes.

The financial side of this problem is contained in the recommendation of a $60,000 appropriation for the proposed dormitory. The appropriation is stated in this amount only because a request for $75,000 (a sum which would give the most economical construction per unit of service, and which would more adequately meet the needs of the situation) might seem somewhat extravagant.

The second immediate need of the University in the matter of building, is an extension of facilities for Engineering shops and laboratories. This year's entering class has in it thirty-three Freshman Engineers, more than doubling the pressure upon already crowded quarters. Also, the excellent plans of Professor Richter for the betterment of our Engineering instruction through the provision of testing laboratories and equipment require additional space for their fulfillment. And it should be understood that this proposed equipment, more extensive than any that has heretofore been provided, is absolutely necessary if our Engineers are to have facilities at all comparable in quality to the reasonable demands of the profession.

Shops and laboratories such as are necessary to meet this situation for the immediate future will cost at least $25,000, and this amount is suggested for an appropriation.

The limited amount of land in the University campus has been a matter of deep concern to all observing friends of the institution. . It takes only a slight acquaintance with the older State Universities, and some reflection upon the University of Montana, to convince any one that its present campus is entirely too small for its future use. The time to buy is right now, before the land adjacent to the present campus passes into the hands of small holders who will build homes and thus cut off expansion, except at very high prices. A due regard for the proprieties of private negotiations permits me to say merely in general terms, that land increasing the size of the campus by about fifty per cent may be purchased at about one-third of its market value for residence lots, if an appropriation of $25,000 can be made available at the coming session of the Legislature.

In the care of the grounds, with its lawns, flowers, shrubbery and trees, it is necessary to keep the campus fenced. About one-third of it is surrounded by an ornamental iron fence. The other two-thirds has a wooden post and board fence which is rotting and falling down in every storm. The main sewer under the circular drive way constantly gives trouble because of the instrusion of roots from shade trees. Cement walks are only imperfectly provided in certain parts of the grounds. For these three matters I recommend an appropriation of $2,000.00.

For two successive years your attention has been called to the total lack of a building for the use of the Biological Station on Flathead Lake. The summer work which should be carried on at the Station is too valuable in its scientific interest to permit its abandonment. An appropriation of $2,000 would provide a simple but satisfactory structure, built lightly for summer use only.

ENDOWMENT AND MAINTENANCE INCOME.

The chief source of income for maintenance of the University has been and is direct appropriation from the General Fund of the State. For the biennium to close February 28th next, this appropriation has been $137,500.

The University also has a landed endowment given by the Federal Government, the income of which is devoted to maintenance. Sales of lands and of timber must be used for a Permanent Fund, to be invested in interest bearing securities. The interest on the Permanent Fund, together with proceeds of leases constitute the Interest and Income Fund.

The summary of these two funds on November 30th, is as follows:

University Permanent Fund

Nov. 30, 1910, Amount of bonds $216,700.00
Nov. 30, 1910, Amount of cash 3,253.35

University Interest and Income Fund.

Nov. 30, 1910, Cash on hand $3,004.36

It will be remembered that the last Legislature passed an act authorizing the issue of $50,000 in bonds to replace in the Interest and Income Fund that amount which had recently been used for the payment of illegal building bonds. The act has not affected the fund, because the authority thus given has not been exercised.

The amount of the Interest and Income Fund audited on maintenance account during the two years ending November 30th, was $22,963.40. By direction of the State Board of Examiners this sum has been treated, not as an addition to the resources of the University, but as a means of leaving unexpended in the General Fund Appropriation an equal sum.

The probable income for the Interest and Income Fund during the next biennium, from February 28, 1911, to February 28, 1913, is about $31,000.

Students registering in the University pay certain general fees, called Matriculation and Athletic fees. These may be estimated at $2,000.00 for 1911-12 and $2,200.00 for 1912-13.

Upon the basis of the recommendations made in preceding sections, and upon the facts just stated about other sources of income, appropriations from the General Fund of $79,000 and $81,800 for the two next succeeding years are needed.

GIFTS TO THE UNIVERSITY

Previous reports have made due acknowledgment of annual gifts of $450 from Senator W. A. Clark for biological and geological summer work. These helpful gifts still contribute to the success of this original scientific research.

The Bonner Scholarship of $300 annually; the Keith Debating Scholarship of $50; the Houston Debating Scholarship of $25; the Bennett Prize of $20; the Buckley Prize of $20; the Cobban Prize of $25; the 1904 Class Prize of $15; the Joyce Memorial Medal; the Mrs. E. L. Bonner Music Medal, continue to confer benefits upon the University.

The most notable gift of the year came from Mr. F. S. Lusk, who presented to the Department of Engineering an electrical equipment which cost $2,500 and had been used during the construction of certain railroad tunnels. The material embraces dynamos and complete apparatus for lighting purposes, which will be of service both experimentally and practically.

Several manufacturers of engineering machinery have made gifts and loans of valuable apparatus for the Department of Engineering.

The University has been favored with the loan of two of his paintings by Mr. E. L. Paxson. The subjects are "Sacajawea" and "Custer's Last Stand." They hang in the Library Building where they are viewed with pleasure by large numbers of visitors.

Donations of several hundred dollars from citizens of Missoula assisted materially last May in meeting the expenses of the Interscholastic Meet.

The Library has received a number of donations of books from individuals, and copies of their newspapers from a large number of Montana publishers.

The Class of 1910 presented a handsome memorial stone seat, which is placed near the main entrance gate.

The several class organizations of students and the Associated Students raised $150 to meet part of the expense of putting a new floor in the Gymnasium. Their interest in the matter came primarily from their use of the Gymnasium for dancing parties, but their public spirit is none the less commendable.

A committee representing the students living in Woman's Hall is taking the lead in raising money to furnish the new Infirmary Cottage for the care of cases of contagious and infectious diseases.

The Alumni Association raised the money for the expense of sending a traveling representative to visit high schools in order to interest recent graduates in the University.

The recapitulation of these matters is valuable in illustrating the point that the habit of giving to the University will surely grow as more and more people come to appreciate its needs. In a thousand ways, in large as well as small enterprises, private benefactions can supplement the support of the state.

THE ALUMNI.

Its graduates are the permanent pride of the University. Their success in their several careers will be taken as evidences of the public service rendered by the institution. Their loyalty is a basis upon which to build the ever-growing University. During the past year the Alumni have given their services cordially in a campaign to bring the University properly before the people. They worked enthusiastically for an increased enrollment, with results already stated. They became centers of influence and activity to advocate the passage of the constitutional amendment to maintain the state's revenues. We know that they can be depended upon to respond whenever called upon for loyal service.

An interesting fact showing the scholarly standing of the University's graduates is that two members of the Class of 1910 are holding graduate scholarships in Eastern institutions. Mr. Robert C. Line was thus honored by Harvard, and Mr. Wilford J. Winninghoff by Massachusetts Institute of Technology.

CERTIFICATES TO TEACH.

The State of Montana continues its injustice to the graduates of its University by discriminating against them in the matter of certificates to teach. Included in a bill which passed the last Legislature was a clause which would have permitted fully qualified graduates of the University to teach in the schools of the state without examination. Governor Norris vetoed the bill on general grounds not connected with the clause in question. Will not this honorable board again recommend (as it has several times) the passage of remedial legislation on this important point?

STUDENT AFFAIRS

On this general subject I can hardly do better than reiterate some general observations made in my report of a year ago. The primary relationship of faculty and students must ever be that of teachers and learners. Yet the academic life of higher institutions introduces elements of sociability, fraternity and sportsmanship, which minister in a high degree to educational efficiency, if properly directed. This is illustrated by the mutuality which prevails in the University between faculty and students in what are commonly known as student affairs. In the administration of the Associated Students, in social gatherings, in literary and scientific societies, in athletic sports, the interest of members of the faculty is only excelled by that of the students themselves. This team play, this helping spirit, in recreation and in sport, has a direct effect upon the intellectual sympathy which characterizes teachers and students. President Angell of Michigan, declared that he was kept young at eighty by life-long contact with young collegians. It is therefore a subject of congratulation that the personal relation is still a strong factor in the life of the University.

Athletic regulations have been the subject of much consideration during the year. A determined and successful effort has been made to maintain reasonable scholarship and clear amateur standing among the members of all competitive teams. Not a few men have been denied the privilege of representing the University in intercollegiate games because they failed to keep up their scholarship. The winning of state championships in football and in track and field games is a proof that good standards do not prevent victories.

RHODES SCHOLARSHIP

Montana failed to send a representative to Oxford this year to enjoy the benefits of a Rhodes Scholarship. No well qualified candidates presented themselves to the Committee of Selection.

For the appointment soon to be made only two candidates have appeared so far as known. One student in the University wrote on the qualifying examinations, but the result is not

—18—

announced. A young man from Montana temporarily resident in Washington, wishes to be considered an applicant. The Committee of Selection consists of President Hamilton, Superintendent Dietrich, and the President of the University.

The representative of the Rhodes Trust, Mr. Parkin, recently paid a visit to the University for the discussion of problems growing out of the administration of the scholarships. It seems likely that the regrettable lack of appreciation of the scholarships may lead to a limitation of the frequency with which they can be awarded in Montana.

NATIONAL EDUCATIONAL MEETINGS

In July last, I attended the meetings of the National Educational Association in Boston. The sessions were in every way successful. Besides programmes of general interest, there were many special departmental discussions of great value. I took part in the work of the Department of Higher Education, serving on the nominating committees of that department and of the general association. For the present year I was elected one of the Vice-Presidents of the Association.

The National Association of State Universities met in Washington on November 14th and 15th. I attended its sessions, taking advantage of the opportunities on the trip to transact business with the Forester of the United States and to visit the Universities of Michigan, Chicago, and Wisconsin.

CHARTER DAY

The next celebration of Charter Day is expected to be held on Friday, February 17, next. On behalf of the Executive Board and the Faculty, I extend your honorable board a cordial invitation to be present. We shall expect to make arrangements to entertain the Legislature at that time.

The principal feature of the Charter Day exercises in 1910 was an able address by the Hon. C. R. Leonard of Butte.

PUBLICATIONS

The issue of bulletins during the year has been as follows:

No. 60—"Courses in Forestry," by Professor J. E. Kirkwood.

No. 61—"Montana Botany Notes," by Marcus E. Jones.

No. 62—"Announcement of the Seventh Annual Interscholastic Meet."

No. 63—"Forestry," Bulletin of Information, by Professor J. E. Kirkwood.

No. 64—"Fifteenth Annual Register."
No. 65—"Extension Courses," Bulletin of Information.
No. 66—Illustrated Booklet.
No. 67—"Montana High School Debating League," by Professor G. F. Reynolds.

Important scientific studies by several members of the Faculty are ready for publication and will be issued as soon as circumstances will permit. Every possible encouragement should be given to the preparation and publication of scholarly monographs.

DATE OF ANNUAL REPORT

With your indulgence I desire to renew the suggestion made in my last annual report that a change in existing law seems desirable with respect to the date of the President's Report. This report (because made in December) covers but three months of the current session of the University, and mostly contains information that would have been more valuable in June in closing the work of one academic year and in the consideration of plans for the ensuing year. Would it not give better results to have complete annual reports in June, and briefer reports of current conditions and recommendations in December? The other institutions under your care have this arrangement and it is not clear that there is any important reason for maintaining a different system for the University.

Respectfully submitted,
C. A. DUNIWAY, President.

APPENDIX I

FINANCIAL MEMORANDA AND STATEMENTS
OF FUNDS AND EXPENDITURES 1908-10

MEMORANDUM OF ESTIMATES FOR COST OF MAINTENANCE, 1911-1912 AND 1912-1913

		1911-12	1912-13
I. THE FACULTY—			
(1)	The President	$ 4,500.00	$ 4,500.00
(2)	Professors	30,100.00	33,600.00
(3)	Assistant Professors	6,200.00	8,000.00
(4)	Instructors	12,500.00	13,000.00
(5)	Assistants	1,500.00	1,500.00
		$54,800.00	$60,600.00
II. THE EMPLOYES—			
(1)	On full time, four	$ 4,250.00	$ 4,250.00
(2)	On part time, four	1,250.00	1,250.00
		$5,500.00	$5,500.00

III. THE DEPARTMENTS—
Equipment, Supplies and Books, for 21 Departments —Botany and Forestry, Biology, Biological Station, Chemistry, Engineering, English, Fine Arts, Geology, History and Economics, Latin and Greek, Law, Library, Literature, Mathematics, Modern Languages, Museum, Music, Philosophy and Education, Physical Culture, Physics, Public Speaking $13,000.00 $12,000.00

IV. GENERAL EXPENSES—
Heat, Water, Light, Printing, Insurance, Supplies, Repairs, Improvements, Labor, Travel, Sundry, Contingent ....$16,700.00 $ 15,900.00

V. SUMMER SCHOOL—

		1911-12	1912-13
(a)	10 Professors, average....$250—$2,500.00		
(b)	6 Instructors, average.... 200— 1,200.00		
(c)	6 Special Lecturers, at.... 100— 600.00		
(d)	Administration and General 700.00	5,000.00	5,000.00

VI. UNIVERSITY EXTENSION—
Lectures and Correspondence Courses............ 1,000.00   1,000.00

	$96,000.00	$100,000.00

MEMORANDUM OF ESTIMATED SOURCES OF INCOME FOR MAINTENANCE, 1911-1912 AND 1912-1913

	1911-12	1912-13
I.—University Interest and Income Fund..............	$15,000.00	$ 16,000.00
II—From general fees of students	2,000.00	2,200.00
III—From Legislative Appropriation, from General Fund of the State	79,000.00	81,800.00
	$96,000.00	$100,000.00

MEMORANDUM OF ESTIMATES OF COST OF BUILD-
INGS AND SPECIAL IMPROVEMENTS,
1911-1912 AND 1912-1913

I—Dormitory for men	$ 60,000.00
II—Shops and Laboratory for Engineering	25,000.00
III—Additional land for campus expansion	25,000.00
IV—Building for Biological Station on Flathead Lake	2,000.00
V—Sewer, Fences, Cement Walks	2,000.00
	$114,000.00

MEMORANDUM OF APPROPRIATIONS (IN ADDITION
TO INTEREST AND INCOME FUND AND ESTI-
MATED FEES) RECOMMENDED TO THE
STATE BOARD OF EDUCATION FOR AP-
PROVAL FOR THE BIENNIUM 1911-1912

I.—For Maintenance:

		1911-12	1912-13
1.	General maintenance and repairs	$ 69,000.00	$ 69,800.00
2.	Establishment and maintenance of Law Department, new	4,000.00	5,000.00
3.	Establishment and maintenance of Summer School, new	5,000.00	5,000.00
4.	Establishment and maintenance of Extension Department, new	1,000.00	1,000.00
	Total Maintenance Appropriations....	79,000.00	81,800.00
	(Also to be used for General Maintenance, (Interest and Income Fund and Fees, (Estimated	17,000.00	18,200.00)
	(Total for Maintenance	$ 96,000.00	$100,000.00)

II.—For Buildings and Special Improvements—

1.	Dormitory for men	$ 30,000.00	$ 30,000.00
2.	Shops and Laboratory for Engineering....	15,000.00	10,000.00
3.	Purchase of land for campus expansion	12,500.00	12,500.00
4.	Building for Biological Station on Flathead Lake	1,000.00	1,000.00
5.	Sewer, Fences, Cement Walks	1,000.00	1,000.00
	Total Special Appropriations	$ 59,500.00	$ 54,500.00

III.—Summary of Appropriations Recommended—

1.	Maintenance—(In addition to estimated Interest and Income Fund and Fees)....	$ 79,000.00	$ 81,800.00
2.	For Buildings and Special Improvements	59,500.00	54,500.00
	Total	$138,500.00	$136,300.00

FINANCIAL STATEMENT OF UNIVERSITY FUNDS FOR THE TWO YEARS ENDING NOVEMBER 30, 1910.

MAINTENANCE AND REPAIRS.

Receipts.

Balance, December 1, 1908	$ 8,584.64
Special Deficiency Appropriation	5,000.00
One Year Appropriation to March 1, 1910	67,500.00
One Year Appropriation to March 1, 1911	70,000.00
Interest and Income Fund (Vouchers for maintenance purposes were paid by warrants drawn by State Auditor on Interest and Income Fund)	22,963.40
	$174,048.04

Disbursements.

Expenditures as shown by analysis, December 1, 1908, to November 30, 1910	$131,401.25
Interest and Income (By ruling of State Board of Examiners Maintenance and Repairs Appropriation remains unexpended in the sum of the amount paid out of Interest and Income Fund)	22,963.40
Balance on hand November 30, 1910	19,683.39
	$174,048.04

LIBRARY FURNITURE AND FIXTURES.

Receipts.

Special Appropriation	$ 7,500.00

Disbursements.

Expenditures as shown by analysis	$ 7,500.00

LIBRARY BOOK.

Receipts.

From Matriculation Fees		$ 2,288.50
Transferred from Sundry Funds:		
Certified Public Accountancy	$115.72	
Office Fines	61.65	
Breakage (Course) Deposits	87.10	264.47
Publisher's Refund		1.10
		$ 3,544.07

Disbursements.

Expenditures as shown by analysis		$ 2,269.95
Balance on hand November 30, 1910		1,284.12
		$ 3,554.07

ATHLETIC FEE.

Receipts.

Balance, December 1, 1908		$ 171.62
From fees		632.50
		$ 804.12

Disbursements.

Expenditures as shown by analysis		$ 301.69
Associated Students for Competitive Sports		106.75
Balance on hand November 30, 1910		395.68
		$ 804.12

CERTIFIED PUBLIC ACCOUNTANCY.

Receipts.

Fees for Certificates		$ 450.00

Disbursements.

Expenditures as shown by analysis		$ 334.28
Transferred to Library Book Fund		115.72
		$ 450.00

SENATOR W. A. CLARK DONATIONS.

Receipts.

From W. A. Clark for Biological Station		$ 500.00
From W. A. Clark for Geological Exploration		400.00
From Somers Lumber Company for damages to boathouse		25.00
		$ 925.00

Disbursements.

Expenditures as shown by analysis		$ 925.00

COURSE DEPOSITS.

Receipts.

Balance December 1, 1908		$ 895.16
Deposits as follows:		
Biology	$403.68	
Chemistry	914.24	
Correspondence	6.00	
Engineering	226.50	
English	52.10	
Fine Arts	31.00	
Forestry	28.31	
Forestry, Short	250.00	
Geology	78.00	
History	56.00	
Library Bulletin Exc.	3.00	
Music	100.00	
Office Fines	20.10	
Physics	138.00	
Physical Culture	15.00	
Psychology	10.00	2,331.93
		$ 3,227.09

Disbursements.

Expenditures as shown by analysis		$ 1,574.55
Transferred to Office Fines	$ 16.00	
Transferred to Library B'tin. Exc.	3.00	
Transferred to Library Book	87.10	106.10
Sundry refunds of deposits to students, not considered as expenditures		316.90
Balance on hand November 30, 1910, distributed in accounts as follows:		
Biology	$276.13	
Chemistry	256.50	
Correspondence	4.00	
Engineering	179.25	
English	31.60	
Fine Arts	31.00	
Forestry	21.31	
Geology	55.25	
History	50.25	
Music	100.00	
Physics	85.40	
Physical Culture	15.00	
Psychology	10.00	
Short Forestry	113.85	1,229.54
		$ 3,227.09

SCHOLARSHIPS AND PRIZES.

	Receipts	Expenditures.	Balance Nov. 30, 1910.
(x) Bennett Prize	$ 57.75	$ 20.00	$ 37.75
Bonner Scholarship	450.00	360.00	90.00
Cobban Prize In Geology	25.00	25.00	....
Houston Debating Sch.	25.00	15.00	10.00
(x) Joyce Memorial Medal	67.00	....	67.00
Keith Debating Sch.	50.00	25.00	25.00
1904 Class Prize	15.00	15.00	....
	$689.75	$460.00	$ 229.75

(x)   Receipts for these funds are derived from investments in bonds.

UNIVERSITY EXTENSION.
Receipts.

From fees for lectures	$	335.17
From fees for correspondence courses		83.00
	$	418.17

Disbursements.

Expenditures as shown by analysis		$ 334.45
Balance on hand November 30, 1910:		
In lecture fund	$ 14.57	
In correspondence courses fund	69.15	83.72
		$ 418.17

WOMAN'S HALL.
Receipts.

Balance December 1, 1908	$	3,315.49
From room rents		1,943.55
Transferred from Woman's Hall Room Account		192.34
	$	5,451.38

Disbursements.

Expenditures as shown by analysis	$	4,179.19
Balance on hand November 30, 1910		1,272.19
	$	5,451.38

WOMAN'S HALL—BOARD.
Receipts.

From board	$	9,248.10
Transferred from room account		448.55
	$	9,696.65

Disbursements.

Expenditures as shown by analysis	$	9,514.79
Balance on hand November 30, 1910		181.86
	$	9,696.65

WOMAN'S HALL—ROOM.
Receipts.
From room rents .... $ 3,169.00

Disbursements
Expenditures as shown by analysis ....$ 2,376.12
Transferred to Woman's Hall account (Reserve) 192.34
Transferred to Woman's Hall—Board account 448.55
Balance on hand November 30, 1910 .... 152.19

$ 3,169.20

LIBRARY BULLETIN EXCHANGE.
Receipts.
Transferred from Course (Breakage) Deposit ....$ 3.00
From sale of bulletins 61.15

$ 64.15
Disbursements.
Balance on hand November 30, 1910 ....$ 64.15

OFFICE FINES.
Receipts.
Transferred from Course (Breakage) Deposit ....$ 16.00
Collections 94.80

$ 110.80
Disbursements.
Transferred to Library Book Fund ....$ 61.65
Balance on hand November 30, 1910 .... 49.15

$ 110.80

SUMMARY OF ANALYSIS OF EXPENDITURES FOR THE TWO YEARS ENDING NOVEMBER 30, 1910.

	3 Months Dec. 1,'08 Mar. 1,'09	12 Months Mar. 1,'09 Mar. 1,'10	9 Months Mar. 1,'10 Dec. 1,'10	Total 2 Years
Maintenance (see detailed analysis below)	$13,584.64	$66,654.37	$51,162.24	$131,401.25
Library Furniture and Fixtures		7,500.00		7,500.00
Library Book		1,399.89	870.06	2,269.95
Athletic Fee	147.34	108.10	46.25	301.69
Certified Public Account.		334.28		334.28
Clark Donation		475.00	450.00	925.00
Course Deposits	149.60	1,108.57	316.38	1,574.55
Scholarships and Prizes		200.00	260.00	460.00
University Extension		110.70	223.75	334.45
Woman's Hall	242.36	2,747.98	1,188.85	4,179.19
Woman's Hall, Board		4,888.34	4,626.45	9,514.79
Woman's Hall, Room		1,208.18	1,167.94	2,376.12
	$14,123.94	$86,735.41	$60,311.92	$161,171.27

ANALYSIS OF EXPENDITURES—MAINTENANCE FUND.

	3 Months	12 Months	9 Months	Total
FACULTY, salaries	$ 9,162.33	$39,288.05	$31,808.51	$ 80,258.89
EMPLOYES, salaries	1,070.59	5,094.53	4,083.94	10,249.06
DEPARTMENTS, (books, equipment, supplies)	1,177.92	5,868.27	4,630.68	11,676.87
GENERAL—				
Advertising	15.88	555.33	331.14	902.35
Contingent			252.25	252.25
Department Supplies		132.37		132.37
Express, Drayage and Freight	69.83	.80		70.63
Gardener's Supplies			306.76	306.76
General	89.36			89.36
Insurance		825.00	323.30	1,148.30
Janitor's Supplies			67.64	67.64
Labor	138.00	850.30	187.45	1,175.75
Office	32.58	596.18	489.82	1,118.58
Printing	116.61	1,831.46	1,678.13	3,626.20
Public Exercises		245.90	277.65	523.55
Repairs and Improvements	37.81	497.90	895.38	1,431.09
Stationery		128.85	179.05	307.90
Steam Plant		413.49	352.06	765.55
Student Employes	517.62	1,240.34	818.95	2,576.91
Sundry		395.04	83.50	478.54
Short Forestry Course		95.72		95.72
Special Repairs and Improvements		1,993.86		1,993.86
Travel, Official	176.74	590.65	457.35	1,224.74
University Extension Lectures		126.93		126.93
Water, Light and Heat	997.37	5,883.40	3,938.68	10,801.45
	$13,584.64	$66,654.37	$51,162.24	$131,401.25

APPENDIX II

SELECTIONS FROM ANNUAL REPORT OF DECEMBER, 1909

SELECTIONS FROM PRESIDENT'S REPORT
OF DECEMBER, 1909

[Since the Annual Report submitted December 1, 1909, was not printed, a few sections from it are here given in order that the most important developments of that year may be recorded in accessible form.]

* * * * * *

RECENT LEGISLATION ON ADMINISTRATION

The session laws of the Eleventh Legislative Assembly include important measures for the government and control of the University, in common with other state institutions, which should be recorded here. Prior to last April the University had been placed under the immediate supervision and control of the State Board of Education, without the intervention of any other board having statutory authority. An informal "Local Executive Committee," with merely advisory and auditing functions, had been in existence in Missoula for thirteen years and had served the University faithfully within its field. That Committee and a University Committee of this State Board, with one member resident in Missoula, assisted the President and Faculty in the management of the institution.

Chapter seventy-three of the Session Laws of 1909 made two notable innovations in the established system. In the first place, the right to control and supervise the University is now to be exercised jointly by the State Board of Examiners and by the State Board of Education.. The first-named board is given financial control, while the Board of Education is vested with general powers of control and management except in financial matters. In the second place, a new Executive Board of three members is created, strictly subordinate to both the State Board of Examiners and the State Board of Education. This Executive Board, composed of the President ex-officio, and two members appointed by the Governor, exercises delegated powers, both financial and educational, and is the active governing body of the institution.

The significant portions of the new law bearing upon this subject are as follows:

"Section 1. The State Board of Education, as now created by law, shall have power and it shall be its duty:

"1. To have the general control and supervision of the University of Montana. * * *

"11. To have, when not otherwise provided by law, control of all books, records, buildings, grounds and other property of the institutions and colleges named in this section.

"12. To choose and appoint a president and faculty for each of the various state institutions named herein, and to fix their compensation. * * *

"13. To confer upon the Executive Board of each of said institutions such authority relative to the immediate control and management, other than financial, and the selection of the faculty, teachers and employes as may be deemed expedient, and may confer upon the President and Faculty such authority relative to the immediate control and management, other than financial, and the selection of teachers and employes as may by said board be deemed for the best interests of said institution.

"Section 2. There shall be an Executive Board, consisting of three members, for each of said institutions, two of whom shall be appointed by the Governor, by and with the advice and consent of the State Board of Education, and the president of such institution shall be ex-officio a member of said board and shall be chairman thereof. At least two of said members shall reside in the county where such institution is located. Said Executive Board shall have such immediate direction and control, other than financial, of the affairs of such institution as may be conferred on such board by the State Board of Education, subject, always, to the supervision and control of the State Board.

"Said Executive Boards shall also have and exercise power and authority in contracting current expenses and in auditing, paying and reporting bills for salaries, or other expenses incurred in connection with such institution, provided, the Board of Examiners may not limit the power of the Executive Board in making expenditures or contracts which in no single instance or for any single purpose does not exceed Two Hundred and Fifty Dollars. All vacancies occurring in the membership of any of said executive boards shall be filled by appointment by the Governor, which appointments shall be referred to the State Board of Education at its first meeting thereafter for confirmation.

"Section X. The ex-officio member of each of said Executive Boards shall hold his office during his continuance as President of such institution, and the two members appointed by the Governor shall hold office for the term of four years from and after the third Monday in April, 1909, unless sooner removed by the Governor or by the State Board of Education; provided, that of the members of the Executive Board first appointed under the provisions of this act, one shall be appointed for the term of two years and one for the term of four years.

Such members shall qualify by taking and filing their oath of office with the State Board of Education.

"Section XIII. The State Board of Examiners of the State of Montana shall have supervision and control of all expenditures of all moneys appropriated or received for the use of said colleges from any and all sources * * * and said State Board of Examiners shall let all contracts, approve all bonds for any and all buildings or improvements, and shall audit all claims * * * but said State Board of Examiners shall have authority to confer upon the Executive Boards of such institutions such power and authority in contracting current expenses and in auditing, paying and reporting bills for salaries or other expenses incurred in connection with said institution as may be deemed by said State Board of Examiners to be to the best interests of said institutions." (Session Laws, 1909, Ch. 73).

POWERS OF THE EXECUTIVE BOARD

The following regulations, passed by the State Board of Education on June 8, 1909, further define the functions and powers of the Executive Board:

"The Executive Board of all State Educational Institutions shall have immediate direction and control of the affairs of such institutions, subject only to the general supervision and control of the State Board of Education, and, as to financial matters, of the State Board of Examiners.

"It is authorized to choose and appoint professors, teachers, instructors, assistants and other employes, for such institutions, who shall serve as such for such time, and receive such compensation as the said Executive Board may prescribe, subject to the approval of the State Board of Education.

"It shall keep such books or cause the same to be kept by its Secretary and Treasurer, or other officer which it shall prescribe, as may be necessary to keep full, true and complete accounts of the moneys received and expended by it in the management of said institutions, and shall make the reports prescribed by Chapter 73, Laws of 1909, and shall furnish the estimates to the State Board of Education and the State Board of Examiners provided by Chapter 120, Laws of 1909."

GENERAL EFFECT OF THE NEW SYSTEM

It is apparent that the immediate government of the University has been assimilated to the forms hitherto used in the other educational institutions of the state, but with the important modification that all Executive Boards are subordinate agents and must depend upon State Boards for their substantive powers.

Upon the financial side this change, in connection with the appointment of a State Accountant, has brought about uniformity in accounting with frequent inspection—a wholly salutary result for the correction of irregularities and the prevention of deficiencies. The working out of the larger problems of financial control of educational institutions by a non-educational board may well be subject of careful consideration. This is suggested with the greater propriety at this time when the administration of the new system has been carried out with success for several months by officers who were sponsors for the legislation. If an ounce of prevention is worth a pound of cure, it is not too early to begin to consider amendments to a system which might, under some future administration, put the higher educational interests of the State in jeopardy through the partisanship of any two out of three members of a politically elected board with complete power of the purse.

Upon the general educational situation, the new legislation can hardly be said to have had an appreciable effect. It may easily be seen that the abolition of almost independent local boards, whose powers were granted by legislative acts, and the creation of subordinate executive boards, might pave the way for co-ordination and even unification of institutions under the jurisdiction of the State Boards. But the extensive delegation of powers to local boards by present practice as yet shows no such tendency.

* * * * * *

REVISION OF COURSE OF STUDY

As foreshadowed in the report of a year ago (1908) the organization of courses of study has been quite changed by recent action of the Faculty. Prior to September of the present year, the prevailing principle of organization was that of the so-called group system. On entering the University a student was obliged to make choice of a group in which to carry on his studies. He found thereupon that all but a small proportion of his work was definitely prescribed. The new plan now being administered combines certain elements of group, elective, and major department systems. A student is not obliged to make choice of a special field of study until the beginning of his Junior year. Until that choice is made his selection of courses must receive the approval of an appointed Faculty adviser. After such decision he is under the jurisdiction of a major professor, who is then permitted within certain limits to prescribe his course. For further definition of these interesting and promising plans, which seem to safeguard reasonable breadth of education while encouraging and even requiring special training in some one field of knowledge, the following statement of requirements and electives is quoted from the Faculty regulations:

REQUIREMENTS FOR GRADUATION

"For graduation a student must complete 122 credit hours of work, including 2 credit hours for required physical culture. One credit hour represents three hours of time each week throughout one semester, occupied in recitations or lectures and in preparation outside of class room.

"Time given to laboratory work is credited on the same basis of valuation, 'three hours for one.'

"Students in the professional schools must complete the work required in those schools, but calculated upon a basis of not less than a total of 122 credit hours. Requirements beyond English composition and physical culture do not apply to them, since professional departments definitely prescribe their work.

REQUIRED AND ELECTIVE WORK

"*Required of all—*
    2 courses in English Composition..............4 to 6 hours
    4 courses in Physical Culture (2 hours
       per week for 2 years).....................2 hours
"*Restricted Electives—*
    2 courses in Science ....6 to 10 hours
    4 courses in Language, other than Eng-
       lish ....12 to 20 hours
    2 courses in History or Economics............6 to 10 hours
    2 courses in Literature or Philosophy.........6 to 10 hours
"*Major Department Electives—*
Not later than the Junior year, every student must choose a major department. This department may command from 30 to 40 hours of the student's time, including the hours in this department taken in the restricted electives given above.. The major professors define their prescriptions for each student.
"*Free Electives—*
The rest of the 122 required hours are entirely free electives. These will be from 58 to 26 hours according to whether the minimum or maximum number of hours are taken in the required subjects, the restricted electives and the major department."

REVISION OF ENTRANCE REQUIREMENTS

Problems in the relations of public high schools and state universities originate mostly in the adjustment of school curricula and university entrance requirements. Herein most educators would agree on certain fundamental general principles. They would admit that high schools do not exist primarily to serve as preparatory departments for universities, but that they have more important self-justification in educational service for the great majority who do not seek collegiate and professional training. Likewise, it would be agreed that universities are not obliged to accept unquestioned the product of every high school without regard to the quality of its work, because the University is able to be effective only if its entrants are trained to profit by its instruction.

Differences of opinion and of policy develop, however, when we turn from these principles to outline courses of study and to define entrance requirements. The ideal condition, scarcely to be realized in practice, might be found in joint commissions of university and high school experts to agree upon satisfactory courses of study and methods of transition to collegiate standing. My purpose is to explain a solution based upon existing institutions in Montana, which has been only recently worked out by the University.

All educational interests of the State are under the supervisory care of an elective State Superintendent of Public Instruction and a State Board of Education mostly appointed by the Governor. Local school boards and county high school boards exercise direct control in their several jurisdictions. But the laws permit the State Board and the State Superintendent to regulate the entrance requirements to high schools, both by proclaiming courses of study for common schools and by conducting uniform examinations for promotion into high schools. As a next step in state wide regulation. the State Board of Education formulates a uniform course of study for accredited high schools. This course of study comprises four groups—Classical, English, Scientific, Commercial—and within each group certain amounts of substitutions or electives are recognized. Again the State Board has appointed the President of the University and the State Superintendent of Public Instruction as Inspectors of High Schools, to see that the administration, the equipment, and the teaching, are actually maintained on good standards.

With this analysis of the situation in mind one can see the rationality of the action of the University in accepting the graduates of any four-year course in accredited high schools, not only without examination, but (and herein lies the new feature of the system) without specification of required subjects. Inasmuch as the same State Board of Education governs or may govern in more or less detail the University, the high schools and the common schools as parts of one great system; since the University furnishes most of the inspection of the work of preparatory training; and because the University binds itself only to accept the products of the official course of study, a policy that might seem to open the door to "educational anarchy" becomes really a logical adjustment for the student and a measure based on the confidence which the University feels in the good faith and the good work of the secondary schools.

A summary statement of the new regulations follows:

GENERAL REQUIREMENTS

"The completion of a four years' preparatory or high school course is the standard for regular entrance to the Freshman class. This must include at least 15 units of work. The term unit of work means one subject pursued for at least 36 weeks with not less than 5 recitations per week, of not less than 40 minutes each.

"Applicants must be at least sixteen years old and must present evidence of good moral character.

"A good preparation for beginning the University work should include in the 15 units the following: 3 or 4 units of Mathematics, 4 units of English, 2 to 4 units of language other than English, 2 units of History, 1 or 2 units of Science.

"Students planning to enter the Department of Engineering should include Physics and four years of Mathematics in their preparation.

ADMISSION ON CERTIFICATES

"Graduates of the accredited high schools of Montana obtain admission by presenting certificates of principals stating subjects taken, time given to each and grades obtained.

"Entrance credit is given for all subjects in the official courses of study for Montana high schools, which are properly certified as having been taken by the applicant. Subjects other than those in the official courses may be recognized for credits upon application in each case.

"Preparatory work done in other schools than those accredited may receive credit. Applicants from such schools should present certificiates stating the same points as those given from accredited schools. Similar blanks are furnished by the University.

"When the evidence of certificates is not clear and satisfactory, examinations will be given.

ADMISSION ON EXAMINATION

"Applicants wishing to receive entrance credits on subjects for which they do not present satisfactory certificates are required to take examinations on days prescribed in the calendar of the University.

CONDITIONAL ADMISSION

"The entrance requirement of the completion of a four years' preparatory course with at least fifteen units of credit, may be modified in individual cases by permitting the conditional admission of students otherwise qualified if they are entitled to at least thirteen admission units.

"Entrance conditions must be removed within one year from time of admission.

"This may be accomplished by private study or tutoring and the passing of entrance examinations; by arranging to take the requisite courses in the regular classes of the Missoula County High School; or by transferring certain University credit hours and counting them toward entrance standing instead of toward graduation.

ADMISSION OF SPECIAL STUDENTS

"Mature persons may be admitted without the usual entrance units as special students, not candidates for degrees, if they give satisfactory evidence that they are prepared to pursue successfully the special courses desired.

"Special students may acquire status as regular students and become candidates for degrees upon complying with the rules applicable to such cases.

ADMISSION TO ADVANCED STANDING

"Students entering from collegiate departments of other colleges and universities must bring certificates of honorable dismissal. Upon presentation of the proper certificates they will receive college credit for courses taken in institutions of approved standards."

*　　　*　　　*　　　*　　　*　　　*

CERTIFIED PUBLIC ACCOUNTANCY

Chapter 39 of the Session Laws of 1909. effective February 17th, 1909, provides for the regulation of the practice of public accounting in this State. The State University administers this law and issues certificates of competency to any person who:

(1) Is a citizen of the United States or who has in good faith and in the manner required by law declared his intention of so becoming.

(2) Is of the age of 21 years.

(3) Is of good moral character.

(4) Is a graduate of an Accredited High School or has had an equivalent education.

(5) Has had three years' practical experience in accounting acquired in practice on his own account, or in the office of a public accountant, or in a responsible accounting position in the employ of a business corporation, firm or individual.

(6) Has successfully passed certain written and oral examinations prescribed by the law, or

(7) Is exempt under the section of the law applicable to persons having certificates of other states or countries, or under the provision for the exemption of experienced accountants now practicing in the state; and

(8) Has paid in advance the fee of twenty-five dollars, as prescribed by the law.

The above mentioned examinations are held at least once each year and at least thirty days' notice of the time and place of holding is given by advertisement in three representative daily newspapers of the State. The first examination will be held December 15th and 16th, 1909, and thereafter annually in December, or semi-annually, in June and December.

The provisions of the law are carried out by:

(a) A University Committee on Accountancy, consisting of Professors J. H. Underwood and L. C. Plant, and President C. A. Duniway.

(b) A Board of Examiners, consisting of three certified public accountants of the State of Montana, appointed by the President of the University. The members of the present Board are: L. G. Peloubet, J. C. Phillips and Donald Arthur (Secretary), of Butte.

Provision is made for the revocation of certificates for unprofessional conduct or other sufficient cause and for the punishment of any person falsely representing himself as being a Certified Public Accountant or as holding such a certificate.

The law fixes the standard of general education required for the certificate and imposes upon the State University the duty of fixing the standard of special and technical education to be required. The University accordingly makes the following statement of its policy for the guidance of practicing accountants:

(a) That, potentially, accountancy is a learned profession.

(b) That, in practice, accountancy has not yet reached the professional plane, but is progressing in that direction.

(c) That educational institutions cannot elevate accountancy to the dignity of a liberal profession without the aid of the practicing accountants themselves, nor can the practicing accountants do so without the aid of the schools.

(d) That the attainment of the professional plane depends, first, upon the establishment by educational institutions of courses covering subjects essential to the highest development of accountancy; and, second, upon the efforts of each practicing accountant to increase and broaden his own education.

(e) The University therefore instructs the Board of Examiners first appointed under the law that the standard of special and technical education now to be adopted shall be fixed by the existing facilities for acquiring an education in accountancy and by the average standard of the body of public accountants at present in practice; and further, that the standard so fixed must be raised from time to time to keep pace with the greater facilities furnished and the advances made by the practicing accountants themselves.

Section four of the law exempts from examination the following applicants:

First, those who hold certificates as "Certified Public Accountants" in another State extending like privileges to this State; provided, that in the opinion of the Board of Examiners the requirements for such certificates are equivalent to the requirements in this State.

Second, those holding similar certificates of another country, the requirements for which are equivalent to those in this State; provided, that the applicant is either a citizen or has declared his intention to become such.

Third, persons of at least twenty-five years of age, whose qualifications are equal to those prescribed for applicants for examination, who are known to the Board of Examiners as competent and skilled accountants; provided, they shall apply for certificates within one hundred and eighty days after the passage of the act.

Under these provisions a total of fourteen certificates have been issued.

CARNEGIE FOUNDATION FOR THE ADVANCEMENT OF TEACHING

Following the action of this board at its meeting one year ago the following resolution was passed by the legislature in February

"WHEREAS, The State Board of Education has given its approval to the applications by this State's institution of higher education for admission to the benefits of the retiring allowance system of the Carnegie Foundation for the Advancement of Teaching;

"AND WHEREAS, The results of the operation of the said system, 'which is an educational agency and not a charity,' will be beneficent in protecting the old age of unselfish public servants and in increasing the efficiency and in upholding the standards of Montana's institutions of higher education;

"AND WHEREAS, The Trustees of the said Foundation have made the consent of State Legislature a necessary condition for the admission of State institutions to the benefits of the Foundation;

"BE IT RESOLVED, by the Senate and House of Representatives of the State of Montana, That the State of Montana hereby authorizes the acceptance of all the rights and privileges of the Carnegie Foundation for the Advancement of Teaching, on behalf of the State's Board of Education and by their several boards of trustees."

The passage of this resolution has not yet been followed by the admission of the University, or any other of the State's institutions, to full participation in the benefits of the Foundation. The trustees are pursuing a policy of careful investigation and conservative action in admitting state institutions. Only a few of the largest and best state universities have yet been accepted, and the others must patiently await full consideration of their status. The University of Montana is not able to meet one of the conditions laid down, namely, the receipt of an annual income of at least $100,000 per year for maintenance. Under these circumstances it is gratifying to the friends of higher education in the State that the pioneer president of the University was granted a retiring allowance last June in recognition of his services for the institution.

APPENDIX III

SELECTIONS FROM REPORTS OF
DEPARTMENTS, DECEMBER, 1910

DEPARTMENT OF LATIN AND GREEK

PROFESSOR W. M. ABER

The following report of enrollment in this department for the year ending November 30, 1910, is respectfully submitted:

SEMESTER BEGINNING FEBRUARY 1.		SEMESTER BEGINNING SEPTEMBER 14.	
Latin II	3	Latin I	13
Latin XII	7	Latin III	4
Latin IX	6	Latin V	1
Greek II	7	Latin XII	8
Greek IV	5	Greek I	12
		Greek III	7
Total	28	Greek IX	6
		Total	51

DEPARTMENT OF ENGLISH AND RHETORIC

PROFESSOR G. F. REYNOLDS

Three kinds of courses, generally speaking, are offered in this department—those in composition, in linguistics, and in the study of special literary forms as illustrative of rhetorical principles.

Of those offered in the current year, English I and II, required of all freshmen, and English III, IV, V, and XIV, are composition courses, in which daily, semi-weekly or weekly themes are required. These are examined by the instructor, returned for correction to the student, and then after re-inspection are placed on file. A large part of the work is done in private conferences held with each student at frequent intervals during the semester.

The other courses, except English 0, required of freshmen failing in English I, and English XI, a technical study of English versification, consider the technique of various important literary forms, the aim being mainly increased appreciation.

Besides conducting these regular courses the department has assisted in the work of the University News Service, the University Play and the High School Debating League. Two courses of Extension Lectures have also been given at Helena, one "Studies in Early Drama," with a registration of fifty; the other "Some Poetry of Today," still in progress, with a registration up to this date of sixty.

The principal need of the department is for a more complete equipment of books, the present appropriation being hardly sufficient for current publications and leaving scarcely anything for the purchase of rarer but equally necessary volumes. The registration for the past year is as follows:

SEMESTER BEGINNING FEBRUARY 1.		SEMESTER BEGINNING SEPTEMBER 14.	
English II, Freshman	41	English I, Freshman	70
English O, Correct Eng.	19	English III, Adv. Comp.	11
English IV, Adv. Comp.	11	English V, Public Address	6
English XIV, Debate	14	English XI, Verse	5
English X, Prose	4		—
English XII, Drama	30	Total	92
Total	119		

DEPARTMENT OF LITERATURE

PROFESSOR FRANCES CORBIN

Since the last report no important changes have been made in the department. Ten courses in English and American literature have been given to students who have elected the work. The greatest need of the department is an increase of library books.

The following is a summary of enrollment:

SEMESTER BEGINNING FEBRUARY 1.		SEMESTER BEGINNING SEPTEMBER 14.	
Literature XII, Browning	13	Literature XI, Wordsworth	10
Literature VI, Milton	7	Literature XIII, Amer. Prose	14
Literature VIII, Carlyle	8	Literature V, Shakespeare	7
Literature VI, Shakespeare	11	Literature VII, 18th Century	6
Literature II, General	5	Literature I, Outlines	10
Literature XIV, Amer. Poets	24		—
	—	Total	40
Total	68		

DEPARTMENT OF PUBLIC SPEAKING

INSTRUCTOR MABEL R. SMITH

The Department of Public Speaking is at present offering two courses—Elementary Speaking and Oratory.

The aim of the elementary course is to make the students distinct speakers, good readers of the useful styles of literature.

The course in oratory aims to make the student familiar with the best models in oratory, give him an easy appearance on the platform, help him to be easy and natural in extemporaneous speaking.

A text book is used as foundation for work in Public Speaking, but much of the work is done from standard books selected from library.

The following is a summary of class enrollment:

<table>
<tr><td colspan="2">SEMESTER BEGINNING FEBRUARY 1.</td><td colspan="2">SEMESTER BEGINNING SEPTEMBER 14.</td></tr>
<tr><td>Elementary</td><td>11</td><td>Elementary</td><td>17</td></tr>
<tr><td>Oratory</td><td>6</td><td>Oratory</td><td>5</td></tr>
<tr><td>Total</td><td>17</td><td>Total</td><td>22</td></tr>
</table>

DEPARTMENT OF MODERN LANGUAGES

PROFESSOR F. C. SCHEUCH

The following report of enrollment in this department for the year ending November 30, 1910, is respectfully submitted:

<table>
<tr><td colspan="2">SEMESTER BEGINNING FEBRUARY 1.</td><td colspan="2">SEMESTER BEGINNING SEPTEMBER 14.</td></tr>
<tr><td>German II</td><td>18</td><td>German I</td><td>6</td></tr>
<tr><td>French II</td><td>24</td><td>German III</td><td>18</td></tr>
<tr><td>German IV</td><td>8</td><td>French I</td><td>30</td></tr>
<tr><td>French IV</td><td>12</td><td>French III</td><td>16</td></tr>
<tr><td>German VI</td><td>13</td><td>German V</td><td>6</td></tr>
<tr><td>French VI</td><td>9</td><td>German VII</td><td>5</td></tr>
<tr><td>German VIII</td><td>10</td><td>Spanish I</td><td>7</td></tr>
<tr><td>French VIII</td><td>5</td><td>Spanish III</td><td>4</td></tr>
<tr><td>French (Special)</td><td>4</td><td></td><td></td></tr>
<tr><td>Spanish II</td><td>10</td><td>Total</td><td>92</td></tr>
<tr><td>Spanish III</td><td>2</td><td></td><td></td></tr>
<tr><td>Total</td><td>114</td><td></td><td></td></tr>
</table>

DEPARTMENT OF PHILOSOPHY AND EDUCATION

PROFESSOR W. F. BOOK

This department has been much strengthened by the appointment at the beginning of the present collegiate year of Dr. J. H. Stoutemyer, as instructor of History and Education. With his assistance, the work as formerly outlined by the department can be carried on in a much more satisfactory manner than before. Besides facilitating the work at the University, it has enabled the head of the department to take part in the county institutes of the state. He has this year worked as a regular instructor in six counties, giving in all thirty-nine regular lectures, four evening addresses and several informal talks. This kind of work can be made very helpful both to the teachers of the state and to the

University. The work at the University has in no way suffered by the work.

The head of the department has published, since the last annual report, two scientific studies, "The Role of the Teacher in the Most Expeditious and Economic Learning," *Journal of Educational Psychology*, April, 1910; "On the Genesis and Development of Conscious Attitudes, (Bewustseinslagen)." *Psychological Review*, November, 1910. He is at present making a psychological study of Mental Adaption and colaborating and bringing together what is known about the Psychology of Learning, a work which he hopes to complete during the next two years.

SOME NEEDED IMPROVEMENTS

1. There is needed an immediate considerable expenditure for apparatus and books to put the Department of Philosophy and Education on its feet. It is disheartening to a man to have to hunt around for courses to give to fit limited apparatus and books.

2. There have been collected during the year copies of the reports of all the state commissioners of education, the yearly or biennial reports of the superintendents and boards of education of the larger cities, the publications of all educational societies of the country, the school laws of the several states, the catalogues of the leading universities of the world, and about one hundred new books from publishers illustrating the application of the newer methods to the work of the school. Seven of the eleven departments of this Pedagogical Museum have not yet been started and there should be a yearly appropriation to secure the best books on method and the standard studies in education needed by the teachers of the state and the students of education in the University. This museum can and should be made a telling educational instrument in this state.

3. The work of the department should be much enlarged. Two psychological specialists should be added to the University faculty, whose business it would be to investigate all the problems of learning and such other educational problems as would help make the public schools of this state the best in the land. If the University does not take up this work at once, it is neglecting perhaps its greatest opportunity to serve the people of this state. We should do for Education and the teachers of our public schools what Agricultural Colleges and Departments of Agriculture are doing for the farmers of this country, investigate by the best scientific method, all problems pertaining to learning and the welfare and possibilities of children. May I not hope

that this work, which will and must be done in the next few years, be taken up by the University?

4. There should also be provided a practice school for those who intend to teach after they have finished their University course. This could be well carried out if Dr. Stoutemyer could give his entire time to Education next year and if the services of superintendents, principals and high school teachers of Missoula could be secured to give courses in administration and special method under the supervision of the director of the practice school. This plan would accomplish four things: (1) It would link the schools and teachers to the University; (2) it would greatly facilitate the work of the department at the University at a small expense; (3) it would enable us to supply the city boards with exceptionally well-trained teachers and officials as vacancies occur; and (4) it would draw the best students from this and other states. We should plan to work with the school officials of Missoula more than we have in the past.

5. If you are intending to have a summer school this year a plan should be carefully worked out whereby we could get the services of at least one superintendent and two or three of the best high school teachers of the state to teach in the Department of Education next summer.. There is need for this kind of work. and it would also help win the respect of the best high school teachers of the state.

6. Last, but not least, there is great need of systematic and concerted work on the problem of school legislation. Superintendent Harmon has several proposals to bring up and if these matters are not carefully planned and worked out in time, we will fail to get some much needed school legislation in Montana this year.

The enrollment by classes for the year covered by this report is as follows:

SEMESTER BEGINNING FEBRUARY 1.		SEMESTER BEGINNING SEPTEMBER 14.	
Experimental Psychology	8	Elementary Psychology	25
Adv. Systematic Psychology	5	Experimental Psychology	11
Experimental Psychology	8	Genetic Psychology	8
Ethics	28	History of Philosophy	5
Principles of Education	14	Logic	7
Hist. and Science of Method	5	History of Education	8
Total	75	Total	64

DEPARTMENT OF HISTORY AND ECONOMICS
PROFESSOR J. H. UNDERWOOD

Since the last report the professor in this department has completed the preparation for publication of a monograph on

"Debtors' Homestead Exemption Laws," done under the auspices of the Carnegie Institution for the Advancement of Science. He has for the fourth time represented the University and the State in the International Conference on State and Local Taxation, and has served on one of the legislative committees of that body. Extension lectures on economic questions have been given in Deer Lodge.

At the beginning of the year 1910-1911 thirteen students reported as major students in history or economics.

Classes and enrollment have been as follows:

SEMESTER BEGINNING FEBRUARY 1.

History VI, American, President Duniway and Professor Underwood....21
History VIII, American Seminar, President Duniway 2
History II, European, Professor Underwood 27
History IV, English, Professor Underwood 8
Economics III, Money and Banking, Professor Underwood 17
Economics VIII, Political Philosophy, Professor Underwood 9
Economics XII, Special, Professor Underwood 2

Total...86

SEMESTER BEGINNING SEPTEMBER 14.

History V, American, President Duniway and Professor Underwood....16
History VII, American Seminar, President Duniway 3
History I, European, Dr. Stoutemyer 16
History III, English, Dr. Stoutemyer 15
Economics I, History, Professor Underwood 17
Economics V, Business, Professor Underwood 20
Economics VII, Sociology, Professor Underwood 5
Economics XI, Seminar, Professor Underwood 4
Economics XIII, Elementary Law, President Duniway and others......18

Total...114

DEPARTMENT OF FINE ARTS

INSTRUCTOR ELOISE KNOWLES

No work was done in this department in the college year 1909-1910, the instructor having leave of absence. In the present term the following courses are being given:

History of Ancient Art, 3 credit hours.

History of Renaissance Painting, 3 credit hours.

Art Appreciation, 3 credit hours. (2 lectures and 1 laboratory period).

Drawing and Painting, 2 credit hours.

The purpose of this department is threefold: First, it is desired in the History of Art courses to treat both from an archeological and an aesthetic point of view, the development

—48—

and phases of art from the earliest time to the present; second, it proposes to inculcate an understanding and an appreciation of the prerequisites of a fine art production. It is especially desired in the course in Art Appreciation to supplement theory and analysis of aesthetic qualities by sufficient actual practical work to establish the reality of those qualities in the student's mind; third, it endeavors to give as cultural subjects, several phases of artistic production, founding the work on such definite principles as to make it as thorough as any scientific laboratory course.

In the colleges of the United States there is no uniform standard as yet in Art instruction. However, last spring a national society was formed, and a definite collegiate standard is sure to follow. In the meantime, having made considerable investigation into the character of courses now given in several colleges and universities, I have based the courses offered upon the present general trend.

There is a very real demand for work in Arts and Crafts. The amount of such work which one person can do thoroughly, and at the same time do justice to the courses in the History of Art, drawing, painting and design, is necessarily limited. An assistant would give the opportunity to expand along this line, if such expansion is desirable.

DEPARTMENT OF MATHEMATICS

PROFESSOR L. C. PLANT

One of the functions of a University is to prepare specialists. A specialist in any branch of science and especially in Mathematics must know past discoveries before he can do intelligent work of an advanced nature. One of the immediate needs of the department is complete sets of a number of leading journals. The departmental appropriation up to the present time has been sufficient only for standard reference books. While these books are necessary, they do not take the place of the above mentioned journals. The department should be able, through its departmental appropriation, to invest in at least one complete set of mathematical journals each year.

At the present time, to my knowledge, there is not a book published which is adapted to the mathematical needs of the forester. The department at spare moments has prepared a few chapters in a correspondence course in mathematics for rangers. There is no doubt but that such a course, if well developed, would be of very great value to several hundred rangers who, at the present time, are quite shut out from all the literature on forest mensuration and surveying.

The subject of Astronomy, which at present is being looked after by the Mathematics Department, should be developed as rapidly as means will permit. A beginning in the way of apparatus needs to be made immediately. Next year Astronomy will be required of those students who elect civil engineering. As an elective subject Astronomy will stand on its own merits.

The immediate needs in way of apparatus for the successful presentation of Astronomy are: A 6-inch telescope with driving clock, circles, etc., or 4-inch telescope similarly equipped. The first of these instruments would always remain useful, while the second would be displaced in course of time. We should have a Balopticon, a piece of apparatus which would prove of great value to a large number of departments, and a supply of slides or photographs.

The enrollment in classes has been as follows:

SEMESTER BEGINNING FEBRUARY 1.		SEMESTER BEGINNING SEPTEMBER 14.	
Mathematics II	15	Mathematics Ia	35
Mathematics IV	11	Mathematics Ib	38
Mathematics XIV	3	Mathematics III	13
Anal. Mechanics V	8	Mathematics V	11
Mechanics VI	9	Mathematics XVII	1
	—	Mathematics XX	1
Total	46		—
		Total	99

DEPARTMENT OF BIOLOGY

PROFESSOR M. J. ELROD

The division of the work of the department by the organization of a Department of Botany and Forestry has greatly increased the facilities offered to students in biological study, and has made possible more extensive courses for study and higher grade of efficiency in student results. The demands by students are largely for courses made interesting and valuable by those having them in charge. The growth and development of modern science makes it impossible for any one to be skilled and expert in several subjects, as was possible a few decades ago. Still further division of the two departments can be made at an early day, with great profit to the University, the students and the State generally.

Class work, accompanied by laboratory practice, requires most of the time and strength. The classes taught during the past fiscal year are as follows: General Biology, four hours credit, throughout the year; Photography, two hours credit, during the year; Advanced Biology, taking up special problems for study, throughout the year; Human Body, second semester; Entomology, first semester. The table giving number of students in each class is appended.

During the year one bulletin has been issued, entitled "Montana Botany Notes," by Marcus E. Jones. The material for the bulletin was secured during his several visits to Montana in connection with the University of Montana Biological Station, and represents only a small part of the work accomplished. A fairly complete report on the flora of the State, with a great deal of new material and data, too valuable to be withheld, is completed and ready for publication. Duplicates of the material reported in this bulletin are in the University herbarium. The bulletin covers seventy-six pages with five illustrations.

Other subjects under investigation are being slowly worked up, the scattered intervals for study, considering the classes provided for and the numerous other duties, making progress slow and often discouraging. Considerable progress has been made in the study of batrachians and reptiles; the study of the life of the lakes of the state has been advanced; a collection of insects and other life has been secured from the "Glacier National Park."

During the year assistance was rendered in preparing material for the State Fair at Helena, and for Missoula and Ravalli county fairs. In addition to the museum and other collections as shown at the fair, a series of transparencies was prepared, showing the buildings and student activities of the University.

The department has for many years freely provided photographs for advertising and other purposes. Practically all the photographs used in University publications, in the student paper, in newspapers where half tones representing the University are used, and largely in the Sentinel, the annual publication by the students, have been prepared by the department, without expense, other than the cost of the material. The annual saving through this assistance is an item of considerable importance, besides the advantage derived from having an abundance of negatives, since all negatives are kept on file. The stock of negatives now numbers between four and five thousand.

Outside of class and University duties considerable help has been rendered in many ways of public service. Assistance has been rendered the Missoula Chamber of Commerce in the preparation of their advertising pamphlet; to the Montana Horticultural Society, through service as secretary and in the preparation of the annual proceedings of the society for publication; and to the public generally through public lectures and articles for the press on various subjects. The department superintends the local weather bureau observations.

Considerable work has been done on the museum collections, located in the library building. The collections are too far removed for advantageous use, or for taking advantage of odd moments in caring for material. Notwithstanding this difficulty much has been done. The Homer Squyer collection of shells, consisting of several thousand species, loaned to the University, has been arranged for exhibition in new cases. The collection of insects has been partly worked over. Over 100 Comstock cases are on display in the museum, besides those in the rooms of the department, or a total of about 150 cases. Besides these about 100 Schmidt cases contain insects not yet arranged for the museum or for permanent collection. The collection of bird skins has been safely disposed of in cases, and is being arranged in orderly series for class use and for study.

The urgent needs of the department are, briefly, as follows:

1. Considerable outlay for library books for advanced students. The present appropriation to the department is consumed in the purchase of supplies and a little new equipment each year, leaving too small an amount for needed reference works. As there is a wide range of study covered by the work of the department, to add to the working library the volumes published from month to month that are essential is impossible, not to mention the large list of important sets.

2. Either more help in teaching should be provided, or the number of classes should be reduced, or less should be done in assisting with affairs outside the class room. The spirit of the times and the progress of the University suggest the first as the best solution.

3. It has been suggested in former reports that the University should, if possible, make arrangements with the United States Government so that the erection of a government building for Weather Bureau Service on the University campus would be possible. At the present time the observations are taken by a student, under the direction of the department, which assumes the responsibility. In the near future the service will doubtless be extended and a weather bureau man permanently employed. For obvious reasons the service should be kept at the University, rather than in some other part of the city. Lectures or courses in Meteorology are of great educational and practical value. What we have we should keep, and add to it if possible.

The proximity of the mountains make possible many interesting and important studies of mountain climatology. Naturally, the University must take the initiative in this matter, and must help our representatives in pushing it along. The authorities of the University are recommended to take action looking toward the consummation of the plan as briefly outlined above.

4. There is great need of a larger fund for museum purchases, as representative collections of marine specimens for exhibition and class use, glass containers for state collections, insect cabinets for the rapidly growing collections of insects, printing labels, student help in arranging and cataloguing, and the like. There is considerable material now in ordinary quart jars which should be transferred to permanent containers.

5. There should be a special appropriation the coming year of $1,000.00 for printing the scientific bulletin now ready for the printer, the same for the year following for publications in preparation.

The number and name of classes during the last fiscal year are given as follows:

SEMESTER BEGINNING FEBRUARY 1.		SEMESTER BEGINNING SEPTEMBER 14.	
General Biology	17	General Biology	16
Zoology	3	Zoology	.14
Photography	3	Entomology	3
Advanced Zoology	5	Photography	5
Human Body	10	Advanced Zoology	5
	—	Advanced Photography	1
Total	38		—
		Total	34

BIOLOGICAL STATION

DIRECTOR MORTON J. ELROD

Owing to the fact that the lease on the land occupied for ten years as a station had long since expired, and the owner wished to use the land, there was no building this year for use of those who might attend the station. A small wooden structure, costing a little over a hundred dollars, was erected in 1899, for use as an outdoor laboratory. The lease was for six years, and the little building was to stay on the ground at the expiration of the lease, as partial compensation for the ground. The building was occupied eleven years. As a result of having no building for use no invitation was extended to prospective students. The time was spent in the field collecting .

The collecting trip included four weeks in Glacier National Park; Dr. Kirkwood spent some time before in visiting different forests and becoming acquainted with forest conditions. The writer spent some time later at Bigfork.

The party on the Glacier National Park trip included Dr. J. E. Kirkwood, of the University, collecting fungi and studying forests; Marcus E. Jones, of Salt Lake City, who had previously spent two seasons in connection with the work of the station, studying systematic botany; Walter Lehman, of Lewistown, and his nephew, photography; and the writer, studying and collecting in Entomology and making a study of the life of the lakes.

The trip embraced visits to territory not seen during the' three previous journeys that have been made to the Park. The trail was followed northward, visiting interesting spots along the way, to Watertown Lake, then westward over Brown Pass, down the North Fork River and east across the mountains to the starting point at Lake McDonald. The places visited are Avalanche Lake and basin, Granite Park, a portion of the Garden Wall, Grinnell Mountain, Swift Current Pass, mountain and glacier, Flattop Mountain, Watertown (Kootenai) Lake, Brown Lake, Brown Pass, Bowman Lake and Lake McDonald.

The pack train consisted of eleven pack and saddle horses. Collecting material included a canvas boat, botany driers, insect nets, a dredge for the lakes, thermometers and hygrometers, cameras and plates, besides provisions and bed clothes.

The collections were extensive, considering the time necessarily taken in travel, and are deposited among the University material. Obviously, at this time of writing, they have been but partially studied.

The contribution of Senator W. A. Clark for assistance in carrying on investigations was used for partial payment of the expenses of this trip.

Citizens of Bigfork are very anxious that the station be continued at that place, and have endeavored to provide a suitable site and laboratory as a home. This place is the best location for a station, owing to the splendid and varied collecting fields in every direction, and also in view of the proximity to railroads. It is to be hoped that they may succeed, but owing to the high prices asked for land adjacent to the lake it is very doubtful if they can succeed.

The people of Polson, at the lower end of Flathead Lake, are anxious that the station should be permanently established at Bull Island, where the University owns 40 acres, on one of its three tracts. They have stated that they would raise a fund for a small building.

Bull Island is between six and seven miles north of Polson, is on the highway of travel, is easily accessible, within easy reach of mail, provisions and supplies, and an admirable camping site. Full report on this and the other two University holdings has been made in a previous report.

The odds and ends of laboratory material from the old site are temporarily stored in Bigfork with Horn and Smith of the Flathead Commercial Company.. The gasoline launch was purchased years ago, was the first gasoline boat on the lake, and has seen twelve years of service. The engine is good, but a new hull will be necessary soon. The row boat was lost on the lake the past season, but it, too, had been in use for twelve years, and had passed its period of greatest usefulness. The tents and camping material are at the University, dried out properly and suitably cared for. Since no funds have been appropriated for material of this nature, the first funds having been raised by subscription, it would seem that an appropriation of $500.00 for equipment, in addition to the appropriation for maintenance, should be made. The station has had a hand to mouth existence from the beginning, and has been kept going by hard work in summer vacations. The station should be put on its feet on a firm basis.

The University of Montana Biological Station is almost land poor. It has 160 acres of land in three tracts, but no building and no funds with which to build. At Yellow Bay it is possible to build a log house from timber on the place, 80 acres. At Bull Island the timber is not of the right character for house logs. The country around Flathead Lake is fast settling up, the Reservation will soon be occupied, in a few years the wilderness will be changed to a rich valley full of prosperous people. The expense to maintain the station is not great, the good it does in many ways is very great. It will be many years before large numbers can be drawn to attendance, but large numbers are not desired. The object sought in establishing the station was to provide a place where some investigations could be carried on, where kindred spirits might meet to work out plans or ideas, and where students could be taught to collect and study material as it is in the field.

It is recommended therefore, that sufficient appropriation be asked to erect a suitable building, purchase a boat or two, fix up the grounds for permanency, and for maintenance from year to year. It will not be difficult to secure help in teaching for expenses, as the new field is exceedingly attractive and alluring and has been worked but little.

DEPARTMENT OF BOTANY AND FORESTRY

PROFESSOR J. E. KIRKWOOD

The work of the Department of Botany and Forestry during the past year has been directed along several lines. First and chiefly, the work of instruction; secondly, development of laboratory facilities and equipment, and thirdly, research. In each of these phases of the work substantial progress has been made.

In the work of instruction courses have been given in Plant Morphology and Physiology, and in Systematic Botany, Dendrology and Silviculture. While the number enrolled in these courses is small, it has doubled since last year.

Besides the regular courses the Short Forestry Course for rangers was given during the months of January, February and March. In this course fifty students were enrolled. Owing, however, to a ruling by the Solicitor which denied the men their salaries and expenses, contrary to the understanding upon which they came, many of them were obliged to discontinue and return to their posts about three weeks after their enrollment. About twenty remained, however, and finished the course at their own expense.

The subjects of instruction in the short course included Dendrology, Silviculture, Geology, Mineralogy, Mathematics, Surveying, Mensuration, Timber Sales, Planting, Grazing and Lumbering, and occupied the men fully throughout the week.

In addition to the above, courses in Silviculture and Dendrology, amounting to thirty lessons, have been given by correspondence.

The schedules of courses as now offered students in the University of Montana will enable our students to acquire good training in the fundamentals of forestry, and should enable such as take it to finish at Yale, Toronto or Michigan Forestry Schools, in one year devoted to a study of the more professional phases of the science.

In accordance with the suggestion of our Committee on the State Fair, this department provided for this year the major part of the University exhibit at Helena, in October. This work involved some time in the preparation of the exhibit which took the form of branches, seedlings, wood sections, photographs and distribution maps of Montana trees, arranged in frames under glass 22x28 inches, and labeled with the common and scientific name of each species. The attendance upon this exhibit involved about a week's time at Helena, and at Hamilton, where it was also shown in part.

The equipment of the department has been largely increased by additions of books, apparatus and material. About thirty-five volumes have been added to the working library, also two hundred and fifty sections of American woods, ten botanical charts, about seventy-five lantern slides, and twenty large wall frames illustrating Montana trees and forests.

About four hundred plants have been added to the herbarium collections, including over sixty specimens beginning the collection of Montana fungi. A system of exchanges has been started with various universities and botanical centers throughout the United States, by which we hope to place in the herbarium of the University of Montana, material illustrative of all the trees and shrubs of the country. In this process much of our cumbersome duplicate material may be eliminated and its place taken by more valuable specimens.

Additional herbarium cases are now under construction, the use of which will double the working collection and make available for study much valuable material which is now kept packed away in boxes.

A nursery is maintained as a means of demonstration and instruction, and as affording material for the solution of certain problems in practical forestry. This nursery, begun about eighteen months ago, was enlarged and extended last spring to over three times its original area. Part of this area is devoted to transplants and part to the sowing of new seeds. About 250,000 seedlings are now growing in the nursery.

The work of the department in relation to research may now be briefly summarized. The investigation of several problems is under way. The reforestation of barren southwestern slopes is being studied by the means of small plantations on Mount Sentinel. These plantations are made matters of accurate record, and in course of time should yield some results of practical value. The natural reforestation of burned areas is another subject to which we are giving attention. Concerning natural reforestation considerable data has been gathered in northwestern Montana and Idaho. The questions of natural and artificial reforestations are the most pressing and important at the present time within the scope of conservation. Most of the last summer vacation season was spent in exploration and study of the forest conditions in northwestern Montana and northern Idaho, and many data in the way of facts, material and photographs were collected.

During the past year several articles have been written on the Guavule, a Mexican desert shrub, of economic importance in the production of rubber. The papers are: The Propagation of

Guayule by Seed; The Growth of Guayule in Relation to the Soil; and the Life History of Parthenium.

The first two of these papers have already been published, the third is in press. Other shorter articles are under way.

The recommendations of the Department for the coming year would be:

1. That liberal allowance be made for the purchase of books, charts, material, etc., partly for purposes of instruction, and partly for study and research, without which no true progress can be made.

2. That greater development of the nursery and reforestation experiments be made possible.

3. That a green-house be erected in the near future, as such a structure is quite essential to the conduct of adequate physiological work in botany and forestry.

DEPARTMENT OF GEOLOGY

PROFESSOR J. P. ROWE

During the past year the Department of Physics and Geology was segregated, forming the Department of Physics and the Department of Geology. While Professor Thompson, the present head of the Department of Physics, practically took charge of all of the work in Physics during the previous year, this segregation has, nevertheless, enabled the head of the Department of Geology to devote his entire time to Geology, and as a result, more courses are now offered, and better work is being done by the students.

The Department of Geology, if increased attendance continues in the future, as it has in the past, will very soon need an instructor. As a matter of fact, it is very difficult for one man to give properly the number of courses that are now being called for. The Department is also very much handicapped for the want of sufficient funds to purchase material, that is very necessary for the courses now offered.

During the year just closing, besides his regular University work, the head of the Department has spent five or six weeks of his summer vacation in the field, studying the Economic Geology of the State. He has written many articles for the Mining World and other scientific magazines. He has also finished writing two books, one, "Practical Mineralogy Simplified," which is published by Messrs. John Wiley & Sons, of New York City, and the other, "Elements of Mineralogy and Crystallography," which is now ready for the press.

Last spring a six weeks' extension lecture course on Geology was given at the Missoula City Library.

The work of the Department at present, for the instructional force, is rather heavy, but good results, however, are being obtained.

The following are the classes organized by the Department and the enrollment in each class:

SEMESTER BEGINNING FEBRUARY 1.

Geology IV, Historical Geology 2
Geology XVI, Economic Geology 11
Geology VI, Physiography 1
Geology XII, Mineralogy 3
Geology XVIII, Adv. Economic Geology 2
Geology XX, Gen. Ore Deposits 3
Geology XXII, Adv. Mineralogy 2
Geology XXIV, Special Adv. Ore Deposits 1
Special Work in Geology and Mineralogy 1
Forestry Geology 50

    Total.. 76

SEMESTER BEGINNING SEPTEMBER 14

Geology I 5
Geology Ia. Engineering 9
Geology V. Physiography 5
Geology VII. Advanced Geology 7
Geology IX. Mineralogy 5
Geology XI. Advanced Mineralogy 3
Advanced Economic Tech. Geology XV 5
Geology XVII. Ore Deposits 4
Geology XII. Blowpipe Analysis 1

    Total 44

DEPARTMENT OF PHYSICS

ASSISTANT PROFESSOR R. N. THOMPSON

During the past year there have been two changes in the courses offered by the Department of Physics. A course in General Physics, III, is planned to follow the first year's course of college Physics, and, with that to constitute a general survey of the subject. A course in Cultural Physics is introduced to meet the needs of students desiring further knowledge of the subject, but not from the technical standpoint. Therefore, this course is non-mathematical. The past year's experience with this course has been so satisfactory that it will be repeated with a request for an increased number of hours credit.

On the whole, the grade of work seems to be better. No small factors in this progress, I take it, are the higher general standards of scholarship requirements and the increased equipment. However, it should be said that our work is still hampered seriously in certain subjects from lack of adequate equipment. For, in experimental sciences, the character and completeness of the equipment have much to do with determining the interest and inspiration to high scholarship in the subject, to say nothing of the completeness of the course.

As the following statistics show, there is, as yet, no demand for advanced work in Physics. The courses taught by the Department and the number of students enrolled in them follow:

SEMESTER BEGINNING FEBRUARY 1.		SEMESTER BEGINNING SEPTEMBER 14	
Physics II	11	Physics I	18
Physics XII	1	*Physics XI	9
Physics XIV	3	Math. I b	18
		Math. XIII	6
Total	15	Total	51

*Physics XI is the same as Engineering VIa.

DEPARTMENT OF CHEMISTRY

PROFESSOR W. D. HARKINS

The Chemistry Department at present has a good body of students engaged in the study of the subject from two points of view, the scientific and the cultural. Chemistry is so essential to our present civilization that it was deemed advisable to offer to non-scientific students a chance to get a survey of its more important facts in a course shorter than that regularly given. The giving of such a cultural course is in accord with the practice of the eastern colleges of the better grade, but was advisable here only because it calls for the expenditure of so little energy in comparison with that necessary for the teaching of the subject from a scientific standpoint. The temptation always comes to a science teacher to make his whole work popular, rather than scientific, directly practical rather than theoretical, for in so doing he makes his department larger and more popular, very largely because the work is easier. That the directly practical work is not truly most practical is shown by the fact that those graduates who go into industrial chemistry with a good theoretical training are the ones who at present get the higher salaries. For these reasons and others it is the present aim of the department to make all of its regular courses strictly scientific and of as high a grade as is possible with the laboratory facilities. It should be said that the chemical laboratories have been very greatly improved during the past two years, and that the work of this year's students shows this improvement, both in the quantity and quality of the students' work. It becomes essential now to build up the equipment by strengthening the spots which are extremely weak, leaving the moderately weak points to be overcome in future years. This subject will be taken up in a later part of the report.

During the year 1909-10 the head of the department was first engaged in research in the Institut fur Physikalische Chemie und Elektrochemie, Karlsruhe, Germany, and was then appointed Research Associate in Physical Chemistry in the Research Laboratory of Physical Chemistry, Massachusetts Institute of Technology. Later in the year he was engaged by the Carnegie Institution of Washington to write a monograph upon the Theory of Solutions, together with the Director of the Laboratory, Dr. A. A. Noyes. On looking over the ground it was found that the present theories are extremely weak in some respects, and that this weakness could be best overcome by certain investigations in regard to the theory of the solubility of salts. Since this was considered more important than the writing of the monograph the nature of the work was changed. The investigations completed during the year are:

The Marsh Test and Excess Potential. The Quantitative Determination of Arsenic. (Journal of the American Chemical Society, May, 1910.)

The Solubility of Salts in Solutions of Other Salts, with Experiments upon the Solubility of Tri-ionic Salts. (Completed but not published).

The following researches were partly completed:

The Relation Between Surface Tension, Electromotive Force and Chemical Action, in a Two-Phase Liquid System, as a Cause of Muscular Motion. (With Professor Fritz Haber.)

A Theoretical Paper on the Solubility of Salts, with Certain Deductions as to the Present Theory of Solutions. (With A. A. Noyes.)

The Free Energy of Formation of Water as Deduced From Electromotive Force Measurements in a System: Mercury, Mercuric Oxide, Hydrogen, Platinum, in Molten Sodium Hydroxide. (With G. N. Lewis.)

A New Method for the Calculation of the Density of Salt Solutions.

The Solubility of Barium Iodate in Solutions of Other Salts, and Certain Applications to the Theory of Quantitative Analysis. (In common with Instructor Hill.)

One paper was published during the year by Mr. Hill and a second is in preparation:

The Hydrolysis of Substituted Acetic Esters. First Paper. Halogen Substituted Esters. (American Journal of Science.)

Second Paper. The Hydrolysis of Cyan-Acetic Ester. (In preparation.)

At the present time no University can have a good reputation among scientific men unless its instructors in science contribute to the scientific journals articles of a strictly scientific character, and to be such they cannot be purely local in scope. The publication of papers just listed will increase the reputation of the University, if they can be completed, and they will do much more than this: that is, the work will make the instructors much more efficient as teachers, and more than all, the true scientific spirit, that of real research, will be instilled in the students. The research chemist is not only more useful to the world than any other chemist, but recent industrial developments have proved that great industrial organizations, such as the General Electric Company, will pay very large salaries to well trained research chemists, and only relatively small ones to technical chemists. It is interesting to note that two of this year's Freshmen have already asked to be allowed to do some research work, and this is not out of the question, especially when we remember the statement of the great chemist Priestley, who said: "Had I known more about Chemistry I would have made fewer great discoveries." In other words, it is better to learn by discovery than to learn by mere learning.

In view of the benefits of these researches to the University, and on account of the great importance of some of them, and further from the fact that the chemistry department is the only one of the older science departments that has never received an appropriation for research, an appropriation for this purpose is asked for the coming fiscal year. It may be well to state that nearly all of this money would be spent for apparatus which will be used in the regular courses of instruction, since the apparatus is badly needed even if the research work is not done. A smaller part of the money would be spent for chemicals.

One of the weakest points in the list of courses for next semester, lies in the laboratory for high temperature work, or what is known as the "Assay laboratory," though this is only a part of its function. Improvements in this laboratory are absolutely necessary, and a special appropriation is asked for. It may be stated that the department is in favor of laboratory fees of from fifteen to twenty dollars per student per semester in this special laboratory, in order to keep the laboratory permanently in good order.

The adjoining states of Idaho, Washington and North Dakota have provided for their Chemistry departments much more complete sets of chemical journals than our own department, with its limited funds has been able to purchase, and if we are to compete with them, as we must, our own department should be enabled to purchase the most essential sets. The fact that a chemistry department has a laboratory does not make its dependence upon a library less than is the case with the literary departments. One point is often forgotten, that the general library is of practically no use so far as chemistry is concerned, while it contains many books of value to the students in all literary subjects. In order that something may be done toward improving conditions in this respect the department asks for an appropriation to aid in the purchase of a set of the Journal of the Chemical Society. This journal contains abstracts of all of the work done in Chemistry, and though we should have the original papers, it is absolutely necessary to have at least abstracts of these papers.

The number of students has nearly doubled since last year, and the number of both students and classes will certainly be much larger next year than at present. There are certain pieces of apparatus which are essential to chemical work, but which the department has never been able to buy. Even if it is possible to buy only a part of these, as many should be purchased as is possible. The department is very badly in need of fourteen platinum crucibles, at least ten of which must be provided for the work in second year chemistry. New weights and balances must be provided for elementary chemistry, which has not been fully equipped in this respect. Details as to the needs of the department will be given in a later estimate.

Amounts asked for Chemistry may seem large, but to the expert in these lines they would seem to be insufficient. That this is true will be seen from the following extract from the report of the Carnegie Foundation for the Advancement of Teaching, Medical Education, by Abraham Flexner, page 129. This great authority in speaking of departments in a University medical school, of which departments chemistry is given as one says: "The budget of a department thus organized in a medical school of, say 250 students, favorably situated, would assign $3,000 to $5,000 to its head, $2,000 to $2,500 to a first assistant, $1,000 to $2,000 additional assistants, $750 to a helper, $2,500 to $5,000 to maintenance, including books, new apparatus, material, animals, etc." (Meaning this much per annum.)

Mr. Hill, who holds the degree of M. S. in Chemistry, and who has done another year's work toward the degree of Ph. D., is assisting in the work of the class in elementary chemistry, and is giving the lectures of the course in the Chemistry of Every Day Life. There is also a large amount of work in the preparation and care of the apparatus which is divided between the members of the department faculty.

The only graduate in Chemistry in the class of 1910 has been appointed Research Assistant in Physical Chemistry in the Massachusetts Institute of Technology, the most promising position which could have been obtained since a number of the assistants and associates from this comparatively new laboratory are already classed among the greatest chemists in the United States. If the University can train only a few great men it will justify all of the expenditures which have been made for it.

The following list gives the number of students in the classes for the year. The number of classes will be increased in the second semester, but, since both of the members of the faculty were unfamiliar with the new laboratory it was deemed best not to give too large a number of courses for the first semester.

SEMESTER BEGINNING FEBRUARY 1.

Chemistry II. General 15
Chemistry VII. Organic.......... 2
Chemistry XVII. Sanitary........ 3
Chemistry XIX 2
Chemistry XXV 1
Chemistry, Special 2
Chemistry XXVI 1

Total................................26

SEMESTER BEGINNING SEPTEMBER 14

Chemistry I. General 40
Chemistry VII. General 7
Chemistry III. Qualitative
  Analysis 4
Chemistry XXXIII. Metal-
  lurgy 1

Total................................52

SCHOOL OF ENGINEERING

PROFESSOR A. W. RICHTER

In order to prepare adequate instruction for the present year, an additional instructor was appointed at the summer meeting of the Board of Education. The increase in the number of students is so large, however, that a further increase in the instructional force is necessary. Under present conditions another instructor or assistant professor should be provided for next year, which instructor would do the engineering work now being done by Mr. Carey of the Mathematics Department. As this man could also do other work, his appointment would afford some temporary relief to the Department.

As it must be expected that there will be an additional increase of students next year, additional shop instruction should be provided for, and the efficiency of the work would be greatly increased by the appointment of a regular shop instructor. I consequently respectfully recommend that a shop instructor be appointed as soon as the necessary funds can be obtained.

I wish to take this opportunity to call attention to the good work which is being done by our new instructors, Professor Shealy and Mr. Plew. Both of these men are good teachers of Engineering and both bring to us expert knowledge in their special line which will be of benefit to our students and the community at large.

SALARIES

It is my opinion that the salaries paid to the Engineering men are not sufficient compensation for the work they are doing, even when taken from a University standpoint. Salaries paid to Engineering men should be as high, and perhaps higher, than those paid in other departments, and it is only by paying men at least a reasonable salary, that the University can expect to keep them. It must be noted in this respect that Missoula is one of the most expensive cities, as regards cost of living, in the United States.

ROOM AND EQUIPMENT

I. Room.

The actual needs of the Department are so great and extensive that it is difficult to point to any one thing as being the greatest until one thinks of the next requirement, which then in turn, is equally pressing.

As we turn to the question of room we are confronted with one of our greatest problems, as there is not sufficient room to conduct our classes. In the regular drawing room two classes are conducted at the same time. The office used by Mr. Plew is also used for a lecture room, a drawing room, and a consultation room. Students who are supposed to be drawing, occasionally must leave the room to permit other work. My own and Professor Shealy's offices are used for such classes as are small enough in number to permit their use.

The laboratory space is entirely inadequate for our needs.

The small space now provided in the basement is entirely unfit for laboratory use as regards space, ventilation and light. It is difficult to conceive of a place where the laboratory work of materials, sanitary engineering and gas engines can be carried on during the present year.

II. Laboratory Work. Electrical Laboratory.

There is great need for electrical measuring instruments, an alternating current generator of 25 or 30 kw. capacity, and a five horsepower electric motor. A new switch board should be provided, as the one now in use is entirely inadequate and also because it does not fulfill the requirements of the Underwriters' rules.

The number of electrical measuring instruments is not sufficient to carry on the elementary work of the course.

A dark room should be provided and equipped for determining the intensity of the light issuing from electric lamps and like apparatus.

III. Steam and Gas Laboratory.

Indicators and other measuring instruments are absolutely necessary to carry on the work in this laboratory. A common slide valve engine, a high speed engine, a hot air engine and an air compressor should be installed.

IV. Materials Laboratory.

For a study of the properties of materials there should be provided a 200,000-pound testing machine and a 10,000-pound testing machine. There should also be a transverse testing machine for testing wooden beams and columns; also a torsion machine and the necessary extensometers and micrometers.

V. Sanitary Engineering Laboratory.

A laboratory should be provided for the study of sanitation and filtration methods.

VI. Surveying.

More surveying instruments will be needed to enable us to carry on the work with the present large Freshman Class. We need more surveying instruments, especially a Dumpy level, steel tapes and a plane table. In case these instruments are not provided there will necessarily be more sections in surveying, requiring additional instruction.

VII. Hydraulic Laboratory.

The Department has no apparatus to illustrate hydraulic work. The need is very great and provision should be made for a hydraulic laboratory. The Missoula river offers opportunities which are not surpassed in any state in the Union. The University is fortunately situated in this respect.

VIII. Shop.

In the shops there is great need for a milling machine and a planer. These tools are present in practically every shop as they are necessary to carry on the daily routine work. Students should become acquainted with their use. Also there is need of more small tools, such as drills, etc.

DONATIONS OF EQUIPMENT

Donations were made to the School of Engineering during the past year as follows:

1. Corliss engine, ammonia compressor, ammonia condenser, brine cooler, etc., comprising refrigerating plant. From Fred W. Wolf Co. Cost to University, $1,450.00; value, $3,000.00.

2. Two electric generators, lamps, wire, switchboard, instruments and supplies. Gift by Mr. F. S. Lusk. Cost to University, nothing; cost, $2,500.00.

3. Air cooled upright gasoline engine. Loan by International Harvester Co. of America. Cost, nothing; value, $100.00.

4. Water cooled horizontal gasoline engine. Loan by International Harvester Co. of America. Cost, nothing; value, $250.00.

5. Model of three cylinder gas engine. Cost, nothing; value, $50.00.

6. Electric watt meters. Cost, nothing; value, $30.00.

7. Services of operator and loan of construction car to transfer machinery to the University. Missoula Light and Water Co. Cost, nothing; value, $50.00.

8. Donation of labor by students in engineering for the erection of a lean-to, foundation, etc. Cost, nothing; value, $200.00.

9. One hundred-foot steel tape, standardized by the United States Bureau of Standards at Washington. Donated by the Lufkin Rule Co., Saginaw, Mich. Cost, nothing; value, $15.00. Total donations, $4,745.00.

NEW COURSES

Following are the new courses offered during the past year:

Engineering	Vd	Materials of Construction.
"	VIIb	Fuels.
"	XIII	Contracts and Specifications.
"	VIIf	Heating and Ventilating.
"	XIIa	Seminar.

The attendance in the several classes is as follows, not including work taken by engineering students in the Departments of English, Physical Culture, Mathematics, Geology. German, French, Economics, Physics, Chemistry and Biology:

SEMESTER BEGINNING FEBRUARY 1

Engineering I b.	Mechanical Drawing	6
Engineering II b.	Shop Work	7
Engineering III b.	Surveying	8
Engineering Surveying (Rangers)		20
Engineering IV a.	Mechanism	6
Engineering IV b.	Valve Gears	9
Engineering V a.	Mechanics	7
Engineering V b.	Mechanics	6
Engineering V c.	Strength of Materials	9
Engineering V d.	Materials of Construction	10
Engineering VI b.	Direct Currents	10
Engineering VI d.	Alternating Currents	2
Engineering VII b.	Central Stations	2
Engineering VIII a. Hydraulics		9
Engineering VIII a. Hydraulic Engineering		2
Engineering VI f.	Electrical Laboratory	2
Engineering VII h.	Steam Laboratory	2
Engineering XIII.	Contracts and Specifications	2
Engineering XII a.	Seminar	2
Engineering VII b.	Power Station Fuels	9
Engineering. Thesis		2

Total 132

SEMESTER BEGINNING SEPTEMBER 14

Engineering I a.	Mechanical Drawing	30
Engineering II a.	Shop Work	28
Engineering I c.	Descriptive Geometry	7
Engineering IV a.	Mechanism	9
Engineering V b.	Mechanics	8
Engineering V c.	Strength of Materials	3
Engineering VI a.	Electrical Measurements	7
Engineering VII a.	Steam and Gas Engines	10
Engineering VI c.	Alternating Currents	6
Engineering VII c.	Thermodynamics	6
Engineering VII f.	Steam Turbines	6
Engineering VIII b.	Hydraulic Engineering	7
Engineering X a.	Structures	6
Engineering X c.	Bridges	3
Engineering IV c.	Machine Design	6
Engineering VII h.	Steam Laboratory	7
Engineering VI f.	Electrical Laboratory	7
Engineering VII j.	Heating and Ventilating	2
Engineering III a.	Surveying	9

Total.. 172

DEPARTMENT OF PHYSICAL CULTURE

DIRECTOR ROBERT H. CARY.

The Department of Physical Culture has charge of all athletics of the University and directs the courses in Gymnasium work. At the beginning and end of each school year a physical examination is given each student and suitable exercises are prescribed for his development. The cards given to each person examined gives him an opportunity to compare his development with that of the average man and also his increase in strength during the year.

As far as possible it is the policy of the department to encourage the men in competitive outdoor sports and while doing such work the men are excused from the regular gymnasium classes. At the beginning of the year about thirty men were engaged in playing football, twenty-five took cross-country running and the remaining thirty were enrolled in gymnastic exercises.

The University requires that each student must have two credits in Physical Culture listed with the total number for the degree. This work is given in the Freshman and Sophomore years, but where the student has a satisfactory reason this may be postponed until a more convenient time. One half a credit a semester is given for the regular gymnasium work and the student is required to spend two hours a week during the semester to receive this credit. This year a new policy was adopted in conducting the gymnasium classes. Instead of having two large classes reporting twice a week as formerly, men are allowed to report any time when they have a vacant hour during the morning and receive individual instruction. This proves of more benefit to the student and allows the Director to spend the time from four to six each afternoon with the athletic teams.

While the gymnasium work and the athletic sports are very closely associated, their basis of operation is quite widely separated. All athletic sports are supported by the Associated Students of the University of Montana, while the gymnasium receives its support from the University funds. The appropriation for the gymnasium is spent in maintaining equipment and purchasing new apparatus. To the present equipment will be added this year, one combination horizontal and vaulting bar, one grip and back dynamometer to be used in making physical examinations, one long horse and fifty steel lockers, to which others will be added next year.

PHYSICAL CULTURE FOR WOMEN

INSTRUCTOR MABEL ROCKWELL SMITH.

Physical examinations have been given all girls, and three classes formed. The work is made more helpful and attractive this year by having music provided for each session. Exercises are given with the special aim of giving the girls ease and grace of movement. The physical examinations show that the girls have good muscular development as a rule, so our chief concern is to give them exercise that will help them to get and maintain a correct and dignified bearing.

The addition of music has made it possible to offer folk games and folk dances, two of the most modern as well as useful forms of gymnasium exercise.

REPORT OF DEAN OF WOMEN

ACTING DEAN, MABEL ROCKWELL SMITH

ENROLLMENT OF WOMEN

For Second Semester, 1909-10......................83
For First Semester, 1910-11.........................72

HOMES

Thirty of the young women are living in Woman's Hall, the others live in their own homes in the city, with friends, or in homes where they assist in the household work.

SELF-SUPPORT

Seven young women are supporting themselves entirely or in part. Two have work in the office, two in the library, one in a home in the city, and two are supporting themselves by tutoring and by making use of their musical skill.

ORGANIZATIONS

The Young Woman's Christian Association has a membership of 25. Miss Hopkins and Miss Gage, district officers, visited the women this fall, and were much pleased with conditions in the University. Three delegates were sent to the State Convention at Deer Lodge.

Clarkia Literary Society is doing good work, and is in a flourishing condition. Programs are held twice each month. The Society has a membership of 42.

There are two national sororities in the University, Kappa

Kappa Gamma and Kappa Alpha Theta. The membership of the former is 10, of the latter 7. The one occupies the suite of rooms on the third floor of Woman's Hall; the other, the suite on the second floor. There is also a local sorority, Sigma Tau Gamma, with a membership of 6.

Penetralia, an honor society, made up of women in the University and faculty, is an organization whose interests are impersonal and non-social, and it is very helpful in promoting the welfare of the women of the institution.

THE WOMAN'S HALL

The Hall is in good condition. Miss Brewer, the matron, is most capable. Three servants are employed and four student helpers. The young women in the Hall are most reliable and an excellent spirit seems to prevail among them.

THE LIBRARY

LIBRARIAN GERTRUDE BUCKHOUS

The year that is just closing has been one of steady growth and reasonable satisfaction.

With the exception of several sets of departmental reports of the Government, all material in the Library is now shelved and properly arranged. The "Congressional Set" has been systematically checked, the duplicates separated, and many missing numbers obtained. Publications of the Bureaus and Divisions have been sorted and placed in pamphlet boxes. The files of six magazines have been completed by the purchase or binding of 250 volumes. It is most desirable that other sets be completed this coming year. It is almost impossible to over-estimate the practical working value of a completed set, as compared with a set which is broken.

More than fifty volumes of state publications were obtained, these mostly parts of sets, and it will be impossible to procure complete files unless it is possible to purchase missing numbers that are no longer to be had from the State librarians. It is most desirable that a considerable sum be expended for law books.

Through the joint efforts of the Department of Philosophy and Education and the Library a large number of State reports on education and sets of text books for the grades and high schools have been collected. This collection, if systematically developed, will soon become a valuable educational library.

The number of books cataloged is double that of the previous year and a large number of pamphlets were classified and the more important ones cataloged. There remains some material, mostly government documents and pamphlets, as yet uncataloged.

Wood shelving has been placed in the basement with a capacity of 1,000 volumes. The shelving space thus provided is practically filled at the present time.

As the University courses expand it is increasingly evident that there are conspicuous breaks in our collection. For the most part these are due to the lack of important treatises and collections and technical periodicals that cannot be purchased with the usual appropriations. If a special appropriation for books and shelving could be obtained the most urgent needs of the Library could be supplied. As agricultural colleges must have experiment stations and the other professional colleges corresponding equipment. so the University should have its special equipment—a library adequate to its needs.

The growth of the student body, the extension of courses and the expansion of the Library have increased the number of books issued for reference and other work to such an extent that, to conduct this work properly, requires practically the entire time of the attendant at the delivery desk. The present system of alternating attendance by various members of the staff is unsatisfactory, and, as this is an important division of the work in the Library, some arrangement should be made whereby it would be possible to have an assistant take charge of the delivery desk for several consecutive hours.

The number of volumes placed on special reserve is so large that the shelving space of the delivery desk is entirely too small and it will be necessary to remodel it.

Before the end of another year the shelving capacity of the stack room will be exhausted.

STATISTICS FOR 1909-1910.

Number of volumes lost 3
Current periodicals—
    Subscription 173
    Gifts of Montana periodicals and others 80
    Other gifts 15
Exchanges—
    Number of volumes received.. 11
    Number of pamphlets received.. 200
Number of volumes bought.. 814
Number of volumes given 322
Total number of volumes accessioned 2136
Number of volumes bound 250
Number of pamphlets accessioned 50

The following donations of books have been made to the Library during the year 1909-1910:

Mr. John H. Inch, Review of Reviews, 2 volumes.

President C. A. Duniway, American Association of Public Accountants, Year Book, 1909.

Miss Eloise Knowles, Architectural history of Glasgow cathedral; Catalogue of the pictures of Ryks-museum.

Mr. C. F. Carey, Gage: The Microscope; Sunset; American Magazine.

Professor A. W. Richter, Sibley Journal of Mechanical Engineering, 6 volumes; Anonymous, Palmer; Life of Alice Freeman Palmer; Cairn: Early English Writers.

Mr. J. Debar, Prohibition.

Mr. R. Nasujima, Lord Ii Nausuke and New Japan.

The following newspapers are being donated to the Library by their respective editors:

Billings Gazette	Miles City Independent
Butte Evening News	Inland Empire
Butte Inter Mountain	Kalispell Bee
Great Falls Leader	Kalispell Times
Missoula Herald	Laurel Sentinel
Daily Missoulian	Livingston Enterprise
Belgrade Journal	Madisonian
Belt Valley Times	Montana Lookout
Big Timber Pioneer	Montana Homestead
Billings Weekly Times	North West Tribune
Chester Signal	Philipsburg Mail
Choteau Acantha	Plainsman
Choteau County Independent	Ravalli Republican
Dillon Examiner	River Press
Dillon Tribune	Rocky Mountain Husbandman
Enterprise	Searchlight
Fergus County Argus	Silver State
Forsyth Times-Journal	The Times
Glendive Independent	Townsend Star
Havre Plaindealer	Treasure State
The Inter Lake	Troy Herald
Western News	Yellowstone Monitor

REPORT OF THE REGISTRAR

For the first three months of the Academic Year, 1910-1911,
September 1, 1910, to December 1, 1910.

REGISTRAR J. B. SPEER.

The report of the Registrar for the first three months of
the Academic Year, 1910-1911, is herewith submitted. Since all
students do not register during the first semester it is obvious
that a full report can not be made at this time. Owing to the
fact that the University has so recently discontinued its preparatory department and has also adopted a system of major subjects
with free and restricted electives true comparisons of registration of students and enrollment in classes can not be made except
to a limited extent with the enrollment of the academic year
ending June 30, 1910.

The total registration to December 1 of the present academic year is 176 in collegiate courses, as compared with a total
of 154 for the entire academic·year ending June 30, 1910, or 145
for the corresponding period of last year. There are 104 men
and 72 women registered up to the present time this year. During both semesters of last year there were 66 men and 88 women
in attendance. These figures do not include 50 students enrolled in the Short Course in Forestry, and those taking special
work in the Summer Biological Station and in the Department
of Music. The registration report at the end of the present academic year will show a remarkable percentage of increase in the
total registration of students, and particularly in the attendance
of men.

SUMMARY OF REGISTRATION

SEPTEMBER 1, 1910 to DECEMBER 1, 1910.

	Men	Women	Total	Old Students	New Students	Total
Graduate	1	2	3	1	2	3
Seniors	17	13	30	29	1	30
Juniors	13	18	31	30	1	31
Sophomores	15	16	31	27	4	31
Freshmen	58	23	81	12	69	81
Totals	104	72	176	99	77	176

SUMMARY OF REGISTRATION

FOR THE ACADEMIC YEAR ENDING JUNE 30, 1910.
(For Comparison)

	Men	Women	Total
Graduate	1	1	2
Seniors	9	21	30
Juniors	21	13	34
Sophomores	13	21	34
Freshmen	22	32	54
Totals	66	88	154

A comparison of "old" and "new" students would be of little value for the reason that many of the freshmen came from the University's preparatory department.

ANALYSIS OF RESIDENCE OF STUDENTS

Broadwater County	1
Cascade County	6
Custer County	1
Deer Lodge County	8
Fergus County	2
Flathead County	4
Granite County	6
Lewis and Clark County	10
Madison County	1
Missoula County	80
Park County	1
Powell County	1
Ravalli County	14
Rosebud County	1
Sanders County	1
Silver Bow County	8
Teton County	5
Valley County	1
Yellowstone County	4
Other States	21
Total	176

	Graduate	Seniors	Juniors	Total
Biology	0	4	1	5
Botany	1	0	1	2
Chemistry	0	1	0	1
Economics	0	4	1	5
Engineering (x)	0	7	8	15
English	1	0	0	1
Forestry	0	1	1	2
Geology	0	4	3	7
History	0	1	4	5
Latin and Greek	0	2	1	3
Literature	0	2	3	5
Library	0	0	1	1
Mathematics	1	0	1	2
Modern Languages	0	4	6	10
Totals	3	30	31	64

(x) Also majors in Engineering:
Sophomores 6
Freshmen 33

Except in the case of Engineering, choice of major subjects is made at the beginning of the Junior year.

CERTIFIED PUBLIC ACCOUNTANCY

SECRETARY DONALD ARTHUR.

The operations of the Board of Examiners in Accountancy during the past year are as follows:

The Board. consisting of Mr. L. G. Peloubet, Mr. J. C. Phillips and Mr. Donald Arthur. held its first meeting in Butte April 16, 1909. Mr. L. G. Peloubet was elected chairman of the Board and Mr. Donald Arthur Secretary. A bulletin containing information regarding the C. P. A. law in the State was prepared by the Board and was issued. under the auspices of the University, to the following: All District Judges. all County Attorneys. all members of the Montana State Society of Public Accountants. all applicants for membership in the above Society, a long list of prospective members, members of the Silver Bow Bar Association, other State Societies of Public Accountants, the officers of the American Association of Public Accountants, High School Principals or Superintendents and many attorneys throughout Montana. Application blanks were also sent to all those whom the Board considered would be interested. During the period C. P. A. certificates were granted to the following applicants in the order in which they appear:

No.	Name
1	Donald Arthur
2	Louis Gervais Peloubet
3	James Childs Phillips
4	Arthur Harry Pogson
5	Percy Walter Pogson
6	Horace Ward Moore
7	S. George Hay
8	William D. Mangam
9	George Raban
10	E. M. Crumrine
11	A. G. Badger
12	John Crawford
13	Arthur J. Andrews
14	J. Lee Rice

The applications received from A. E. Shappee, G. W. Merkle, J. H. Inch, George Raff and John MacNair were not granted as the qualifications advanced in the applications did not meet the requirements of the law.

While many inquiries were received, only one applicant presented himself at the first examination, which was held in Butte, December 15 and 16, 1909. This applicant failed to pass the examination set by the Board.

For the benefit of those desiring a certificate the Board advertised its willingness to hold an extra examination in June, 1910, but, as only one application was received, no examination was held. The next regular examination has already been advertised and will be held December 15 and 16. In addition to advertising this examination letters have been written to gentlemen throughout the state who have at times made inquiries regarding the operation of the law or who, in the opinion of the Board of Examiners, may desire to qualify for this certificate of Certified Public Accountant.

The members of the Board of Examiners in this State have become members of the National Association of Boards of Examiners. This association has been, for some time, collecting information as to the operation of the various C. P. A. laws in the various states, and it is the hope of all the members that in time some degree of uniformity will be obtained in the examinations set in the various states as a result of the work of this Association.

As the University has handled the finance of the Board of Examiners it is unnecessary to report thereon.

www.ingramcontent.com/pod-product-compliance
Lightning Source LLC
Chambersburg PA
CBHW020226090426
42735CB00010B/1603